CORPORATISM AND THE MYTH OF CONSENSUS

Corporatism and the Myth of Consensus

Working hours legislation in Finland in the 1990s

ROGER BOBACKA
University of Aberdeen, Scotland, UK

Routledge
Taylor & Francis Group
LONDON AND NEW YORK

First published 2001 by Darthmouth Publishing Company and Ashgate Publishing

2 Park Square, Milton Park, Abingdon, Oxon OX14 4RN
605 Third Avenue, New York, NY 10017

Routledge is an imprint of the Taylor & Francis Group, an informa business

First issued in paperback 2021

A Library of Congress record exists under LC control number: 00111839

ISBN 13: 978-1-138-71833-3 (hbk)
ISBN 13: 978-0-367-24920-5 (pbk)

Contents

List of Tables

Preface

The book is in eight chapters. After the introduction, which presents a brief contextualisation of contemporary Finnish politics, chapter two concentrates on corporatism in both theoretical and descriptive forms. Since corporatism is largely concerned with representative structures between the state and organised interests, the second aim of chapter two is to focus on consensus building in practice. This approach is concerned with an evaluation of the practical tasks the participants face in building consensus within a corporatist context.

Chapter three examines working hours and interest intermediation in Finland. There are two aims of this chapter. The first one is to evaluate what the development of working hours regulations can tell about the broad picture of interest intermediation on the labour market in Finland. The second aim is a question of whether this points to a model of Finnish labour market policy making.

The aim of chapter four is to provide a contextual overview of working hours as a concept representing current labour market developments. The reason for this is that it is of vital importance to understand the positions of the main economic interest groups when analysing the formulation process in chapter five.

The first aim of chapter five is to focus on how the Finnish working hours issue was discussed, contested and resolved and how consensus on the issue was eventually reached. A second aim of this chapter is to evaluate whether the corporate pluralist arrangements constitute a 'good' polity by reference to the working hours case. The objective of chapter five is therefore to evaluate whether the process has been characterised by participants who have been free from external constraints, equal in the sense that none of them have gained special advantages or disadvantages; and reasonable in their arguments in that they defend them in a way that others have a reason to accept.

In chapter six, the role of the parliament in the decision making process is analysed, including an in-depth evaluation of the role that the parliamentary Committee for Labour Affairs plays in Finnish labour market policy making. The aim is to evaluate whether the Finnish parliament is still as subservient to pressure group influence in the 1990s, when it comes to labour market policy making, as was commonly regarded to be the case in the 1970s. The chapter is divided into three parts. In the first, the formal decision making procedures in parliament are explained. In the second, the parliamentary deliberation of the working hours case is evaluated, and in the third, there is a discussion on whether or not there is a democratic deficit in Finnish labour market policy making.

The objective of chapter seven is to evaluate how the new working hours act has been put into practice and how it has affected the individual workers and employers. This chapter also makes a comparison between a corporate pluralist Finland and a non-corporatist UK. Do the different labour market policies between a highly regulated Finland and an un-regulated UK reflect how working hours are arranged on the shop floors?

Chapter eight evaluates what the working hours case can tell about Finnish labour market policy making in the 1990s. The overall objective is an elaboration on the possible side effects of corporate pluralist arrangements as a means of creating consensus.

Acknowledgements

There are numerous people who have assisted me in the completion of the book, which is also my PhD thesis. Without the help of Kari-Pekka Tiitinen at the University of Helsinki and Esa Lonka at the Ministry of Labour, my empirical material would have been significantly thinner than it turned out to be. Many thanks also to MPs Reijo Lindroos, Anne Huotari, Raimo Tiilikainen, Kari Kantalainen, Armas Komi and Outi Siimes for invaluable information about the parliamentary Committee for Labour Affairs.

The Nordic Policy Studies Centre and the Department of Politics and International Relations at the University of Aberdeen has provided me with excellent support when it comes to travel costs and a hospitable environment. The greatest thanks goes to my adviser David Arter, who supported me with both critical comments and supporting advice. Without him, the completion of the thesis would still be in the future. Many thanks also to Grant Jordan for his supportive comments from a non-Finnish perspective.

The book is dedicated to my wife Morag. She spent many hours checking my non-standard use of the English language, urging me to go on although I was ready to call it a day. She has convinced me that there is also life after completing a PhD thesis.

Roger Bobacka
Old Aberdeen

List of Abbreviations

AKAVA	Confederation of Unions for Academic Professionals in Finland
CBI	Confederation of British Industry
ECJ	European Court of Justice
EMU	European Monetary Union
ETUC	European Trade Union Confederation
EU	European Union
EVA	Centre for Finnish Business and Policy Studies
FCMA	Treaty of Friendship, Co-operation and Mutual Assistance
FNV	The Netherland's Trade Union Confederation
ILO	International Labour Organisation
KT	Commission for Local Authority Employers, Finland
LO	Confederation of Trade Unions, Sweden
MP	Member of Parliament
MTK	Confederation of Farmers and Forestry Owners, Finland
OECD	Organisation for Economic Co-operation and Development
PSI	Policy Studies Institute
SAF	Swedish Federation of Employers
SAK	Central Organisation of Finnish Trade Unions
SDP	Social Democratic Party
SFP	Swedish People's Party, Finland
SKDL	Finnish People's Democratic League
STK	National Employers' Federation, Finland (1907-1992)
STTK	Finnish Confederation of Salaried Employees
SY	Federation of Finnish Enterprises
TPSL	Social Democratic League in Finland
TT	Confederation of Finnish Industry and Employers (1992-)
TUC	Trades Union Congress, Great Britain
VTML	Department of Public Personnel Management, Finland

1 Introduction

This book represents a case study of one of the most central features of the labour market – working hours. Before the industrialisation era started in Europe in the late eighteenth and early nineteenth centuries, working hours had to a large extent been dictated by the cycles of the seasons of nature. The industrialisation era brought in new insights to the concept of working hours through the growing use of machines in production. A common assumption among owners of industrial companies became that production could be increased by increasing the number of working hours. The time spent at work for industrial workers therefore became largely dictated by the operating hours of machines, resulting in a significant increase in the length of working hours. The use of children in industrial production was also common, and they usually worked the same number of hours as adults. The first demands for working hour regulations were therefore based on a need for shortened working hours for children, prompted by needs to secure their safety and health. The result was that, in England, for example, the first working hour reguation was enacted in 1847, limiting work for children (and women) in the textile industry to ten hours daily. In Finland, the first working hours regulation was enacted in 1868, setting the minimum age of workers to 12 years of age.[1] The first regulation for adults in Finland was enacted in 1909 (act on work in bakeries), and in 1917, the parliament enacted a general law on eight-hour working days.[2]

Although the initial working hour problems, caused by concerns for worker's safety and health, have to a high extent been resolved in Western democracies, it does not mean that working hours have become unproblematic by the twenty-first century. Recent changes of Finnish, and Western, labour markets over the last decades have created new working hour problems. There are several reasons for this. National economies and

---

[1] Tiitinen et al. 1996, 6.

[2] Subsequent separate working hours acts have been made. For example the working hours act for shops and offices (1919); a revised act for work in bakeries (1928); the act for work at sea (1924); the act for agricultural work (1970); and the act for janitors (1970). (Tiitinen et al. 1996, 8-9.)

labour markets have become increasingly dependent on foreign investments and international trade outlooks, and thereby also increasingly exposed to global economic trends. A growing service sector, coupled with the computerisation of work, has meant that traditional factory-workers have been replaced to a high extent by workers occupied in service and information. Changing labour markets have consequently led to the need for more flexible labour market regulations when old regulations have been seen as outdated and not corresponding to the new conditions.

In a European context, the European Union (EU) underlined the importance of working hours by its working time directive in 1993. The objective of the directive was to make a contribution towards improvements of working and living conditions in Europe and the most important paragraph in the directive was the statement of an upper limit of 48 hour working weeks.[1] The European Commission furthermore issued a statement 25.11.1998 on how to reorganise work. In the statement, the Commission stressed that education and working hours were central to the development of flexibility and security in future workplaces in Europe.[2] Working hours have therefore become, apart from unemployment, the most important labour market issue in the EU, as well as in individual European countries. For example, in Germany, a reduction of working hours has been implemented in branch level collective agreements as a means of creating employment. In Denmark, a new labour market reform, which included aspects of flexible working hours, was introduced in 1994. In France, a new, and controversial, working hours act was enacted by parliament in 1998 (loi Aubry). The main objective of the new act was to reduce the regular weekly amount of working hours in medium sized and large companies from 39 hours to 35 by January 2000, and in companies with

---

[1] Council Directive 93/104/EC, 23.11.1993. The directive aimed at a practical contribution towards a 'social policy dimension' of the EU. EU social policy is based on a promotion of health and safety, working conditions, information and consultation of workers, equality between men and women and an integration of those excluded from the labour market (EU-Factsheet 1997). In 1998 the European Commission published a white paper to ensure that the health and safety of the sectors that were left outside the original working time directive would be safeguarded in its member countries. The excluded sectors were road, rail, urban, inland, air and sea transport as well as sea fishing, other work at sea and doctors in training. The Commission also published a green paper which was concerned with on the one hand flexibility and on the other hand the relationship between working hours and the creation of employment.

[2] SAK Työelämätieto 2/98, 6-7.

less than 20 employees by January 2002. Great Britain implemented the EU working time directive in 1998.[1]

In Finland, it was mainly the employers who, by the late 1980s, expressed demands for a revision of the working hours act. The problem for them had become how to create more flexible (non-standard) working hour arrangements in order to keep up with increasing demands by companies for profitability, effectiveness and competitiveness. They regarded the regulations in the working hours act as being outdated. (The main problem for workers had been new requirements for flexible working hours according to individual life styles.) The 1987-91 government, under leadership of the Conservative Party, brought up the need for a revised working hours act in its governmental programme, which outlined its main policy measures for its term in office. The following government, led by the Centre Party, in its programme also mentioned the necessity of a revision of the act. The main objective behind the revision was to unify a significant number of old regulations on working hours into one act and to make this revised act more up to date with the new labour market conditions that required more flexible individualised arrangements. A complementary reason was that Finland became a member of the European Union (EU) in 1995 and consequently had to implement the EU working time directive.

The examination of the revision of the working hours legislation is interesting from a political science point of view because of at least the following two reasons. First of all, working hours represent something that is of central relevance to a large part of the public. This poses interesting questions about democracy and how collective labour market decisions were made on behalf of the public in Finland in the 1990s. Secondly, when it comes to revisions of labour market legislation in Finland, the main economic interest groups have had an 'automatic' access to the formulating stages of the processes. Their knowledge of labour market conditions, as well as their representative function for employers and workers, has justified their participation. At the beginning of the 1980s, around 67 per cent of the Finnish workforce were members of trade unions. High

[1] The British government initially challenged the validity of the EU working hours directive, arguing that it was related to workers rights, rather than health and safety. According to the British government, the directive was therefore not to be implemented in the UK, since it had not yet in 1993 signed the European Union's Social Chapter. The European Court of Justice (ECJ) ruled against the UK government, and the working hours directive was eventually implemented by the new Labour government through the new working time regulation in 1998.

unemployment in the early 1990s meant that membership rose to over 80 per cent, a level which has been maintained. Membership in trade unions in Finland is consequently among the highest in Europe. In Sweden, trade union membership is slightly higher, and in Denmark, similar to that of Finland.[1] There are currently 83 different trade unions in Finland, organised into three central confederations (main economic interest groups). The following table lists the current main economic interest groups in Finland.

Table 1.1 Main economic interest groups in Finland 1.1.2000

Central Trade Union Organisations	Abbreviation	Members
The Central Organisation of Finnish Trade Unions	SAK	1,073,800
Finnish Confederation of Salaried Employees	STTK	643,300
The Confederation of Unions for Academic Professionals	AKAVA	375,200
Central Business Organisations	**Abbreviation**	**Employees***
The Confederation of Industry and Employers	TT	470,000
The Federation of Finnish Enterprises	SY	380,000
Public Sector Organisations	**Abbreviation**	**Employees****
Department of Public Personnel Management	VTML	129,000
Commission for Local Authority Employers	KT	416,000

* The number of employees working for enterprises who are members of the Central Business Organisations
** The number of employees working for the municipalities or state sector

Source: Internet homepages of the organisations

SAK is the largest confederation and it represents blue collar workers in both industry, private services, local government, the state sector and transport. The second largest confederation, representing employees, is STTK. It represents white collar workers in the health sector, local

[1] Helsingin Sanomat 10.7.1998.

government, the state sector, services and specialised occupations. The third largest, AKAVA, represents employees with university-level or other equivalent levels of education. The majority of AKAVA members work in the public sector. On the employers side the largest organisation is TT, which mainly represents the industry. The second largest organisation is SY, which represents small and medium sized enterprises. The position of SY differs from the others, however. It has not yet been allowed to take part in the discussions around incomes policy settlements because it has not taken part in the making of any collective agreements. It has instead functioned as a lobbying organisation for its members.[1] In the public sector, VTML represents the state government as employer and KT represents the municipalities as employers.

The inclusion of the main economic interest groups into labour market policy making means that the development of the working hours legislation represents one the most important aspect of political science – the relationship between different groups in society and the state. In a Finnish context, this is represented by a close relationship between the main economic interest groups and governments.

The present system of labour market policy making in Finland dates back to the political developments of the 1960s, where the significance of 1966 stands in sharp contrast to the conflicts that had characterised the first two post-war decades. Despite a strong support for the radical leftist party, anti-communist sentiments had been common at the end of the 1940s and in the 1950s. Ideologically, the Social Democrats had started to identify with their European counterparts and a new party programme in 1952, replacing the previous one from 1903 (which had stressed class conflict) put emphasis on a planned economy and opposition to communism. An ideological conflict among Social Democrats became inevitable and the Social Democratic Party (SDP) began to disintegrate. Left wing splinter groups, both within the Party, and the Central Confederation of Trade Unions (SAK), formed their own party in 1959 and central confederation in 1960 respectively. As a result, SDP scored its lowest ever support of 19.5 per cent in the 1962 parliamentary election. Anti-Communist sentiments among Social Democrats nonetheless faded in the 1960s, and the Party started to support the official foreign policy line, which had been based on

---

[1] SY is nonetheless seeking authorisation from its members to take part in upcoming negotiations on broad-based incomes policy settlements. This authorisation has been regarded as necessary by the other main economic interest groups in order for SY to get a seat at the incomes policy settlement negotiations. (SY statement spring 1999.)

a conciliatory approach against the Soviet Union. In addition, a moderate wing of the radical leftist party started to seek more co-operation with SDP in order to work for welfare reforms.

After the parliamentary election in 1966, the left-wing parties gained a majority of seats for the first time since the second world war. The coalition government formed after the election had a Social Democratic prime minister, and for the first time since 1948, included radical leftists as part of the umbrella organisation, the Finnish Peoples' Democratic League (SKDL). Other members of the government were the Social Democratic League (TPSL), a splinter group of the Social Democratic Party (SDP), and the Centre Party (formerly known as the Agrarian Party). The composition of the coalition was exceptional for Europe in the 1960s, because communists did not gain access to government in another Western European country before 1981 in France. The participation of radical leftists in Finland was not an isolated case, and they became regular participants in governments during the 1970s. The Social Democrats furthermore started to play a pivotal role in Finnish governments after they received the prime minister post in 1966. This is underlined by the fact that between 27.5.1966 and 31.12.1999, the post of prime minister has been held by a Social Democrat for a total of 21 years and 11 months, an Agrarian for six years and nine months, a Conservative for four years and an independent caretaker for 11 months.

1966 was not only significant from a political party perspective, but also witnessed a significant change in consultation procedures between top-level representatives of the main economic interest groups and the government. An Economic Council had been set up in 1955, replacing a previous council from 1920. The task of the renewed council was to formulate methods for keeping the Finnish economy in balance and to promote growth. The council consisted of representatives of the main economic interest groups and the government. It met only occasionally in the 1950s, however, due to the turbulent political climate in Finland. (Between 1950 and 1966, for example, there were no less than twenty different coalition governments). A law enforcing the permanent establishment of the council was enacted by parliament in 1966, and it became an arena for regular consultation between interest groups and the government on important economic and labour market issues. It became a forum for discussion and information exchange, but had no formal decision making power. The task of the council was to make recommendations on economic policy, employment, standards of living, prices and trade issues. It was led by the prime minister and it was the government who defined its tasks in more detail according to contemporary economic and labour market requirements. Between 1966-69 the council produced several reports on Finland's economic prospects, and these prepared the ground for the first broad-based national incomes policy settlement.[1]

Yet, although the council was established and met regularly, it cannot be regarded as important as its Dutch counterpart: The Social and Economic Council. The Dutch council could, with a two-thirds majority, make rules with legislative force for the industry. These rules could, however, be overturned by Cabinet veto. The Cabinet was nonetheless formally required to seek advice from the Council on all proposed social and economic measures. When the Council was united on an issue, both the Cabinet and parliament were largely bound by its advice.[2]

The Finnish counterpart had no such powers, but was rather more of a forum for the main economic interest groups and governments to express their views on economic and labour market policy.[3] The Finnish council was closer to the short-lived British National Economic Development Council. It was a forum for negotiations between the main economic interest groups, government ministers and civil servants, but it had no formal decision making power.[4] The Finnish council has proved to be long-lived, and it still functions as a forum for monthly discussions between the main economic interest groups and the government.

The established consultation procedures between top-level representatives of interest groups and the government also had an effect on economic policy making after the mid-1960s. Up to the mid-1960s, economic policy making in Finland had largely been based on devaluations of the currency in the name of industrial competitiveness. In 1967, the currency was devalued by 31 per cent as a measure in fighting an economic recession and to stimulate exports. In order to maintain the advantages the devaluation brought, strong economic policy measures on inflation and employment were needed. The government, under Social Democratic leadership, was able to reach an agreement with the main economic interest groups and the first broad-based incomes policy settlement was eventually signed in 1968, covering farmers, workers and business. It contained measures on taxation, a harmonised wage-policy, social policy, pensions and agriculture. Although the first settlement was in force for only two

---

[1] Tiihonen 1990, 49-52; Leppänen 1998, 1.

[2] Lijphart 1968, 113-114.

[3] Leppänen 18.5.1998.

[4] Kavanagh 1985, 166-167.

years, it nonetheless set a precedent for decades to come. Policy concertation between the state and the main economic interest groups became an important feature of Finnish policy making. The difference between the pre-1966 and post-1966 situation was that in the latter period the main economic interest groups became more involved in the *implementation* of welfare policies through these settlements, not merely involved as advisers on different boards and committees. The tasks of the interest groups were to moderate wage increases, and in exchange, the government introduced, among other things, a social legislative package where social security and pensions for employees were improved.[1] Discussions on national income policy systems was not unique to Finland in the 1960s, however. Thus, when the Labour Party came to power in Great Britain in 1964 it actively tried to implement an incomes policy. An internal debate about socialism within the party, coupled with a trade union movement still highly characterised by class feelings, led to the abandoning of any incomes policy settlements. The government had to surrender to wage expectations by the trade unions and the business sector lost confidence in it. During the rest of the 1960s all plans for introducing any broad-based incomes policy plans in Great Britain were consequently abandoned.[2]

After 1966, Finnish politics and policy making slowly moved towards a new era of co-operation. The central confederation of trade unions (SAK) was in principle united in 1966, although the splinter group did not formally join the confederation until 1969. In addition, membership rates in trade unions increased sharply from around 350,000 members in 1960 (30 per cent of the working population) to 930,000 in 1970 (60 per cent of the working population). Most members of the Social Democratic League had rejoined the SDP in the late 1960s, although the League did not officially do so until 1973. After the introduction of the first broad-based incomes policy settlement in 1968, no important economic or labour market decisions between 1968 and the mid-1970s could be made without the involvement of the main economic interest groups, let alone against their preferences.[3] Important social, economic and labour market decisions were from now on made as 'packages' through negotiations, bargaining and compromises.

---

1 Myllymäki 1979, 196.

2 Middlemas 1979, 434-437.

3 Myllymäki 1979, 209.

The introduction of broad-based national income policy settlements from 1968 onwards also indicated that Finland was moving towards a system of a quasi-corporatism or corporate pluralism. Corporatism basically concerns the theoretical relationships between states and organised interests. The difference between corporatism and corporate pluralism relates to different authors' use of the concepts. Whilst corporatism largely denotes a theoretical relationship, corporate pluralism relates to Rokkan's (1966) use of the concept as depicting the special relationship in a Norwegian context. (The concepts will be discussed in chapter two). The wide ranging incomes policy settlements in Finland, including vast social and economic policy issues, could be seen as a complementary channel to the parliamentary one. The relationship between these two channels was one of mutual co-existence, where the continuance of the incomes policy system was seen as contingent on the so-called red-green governing coalition between SDP and the Centre Party. Essential changes in power relations between political parties could therefore lead to problems in concluding the settlements. For example, in 1977, negotiations between a coalition government led by the Centre Party, and the main economic interest groups became increasingly difficult, with the result that no incomes policy settlement was implemented for 1977-78.[1] A similar situation occurred in 1993, when a centre led government, according to SAK, led too 'employer-friendly' economic policies in its attempts to bring Finland out of an economic recession. After the government proposed cuts in unemployment benefits, the central confederations of trade unions even threatened with a general strike in 1993. In order to avert the strike, the government had to go back on its intended policies and the threat of strike was eventually withdrawn. As a result, no broad-based settlement was concluded for 1994-95. (For a list of all incomes policy settlements, see appendix.)

Compared to the conflictual politics of the 1940-50s, the development after 1968 consequently became characterised more by co-operation. By the early 1980s, there were, however, still some conflictual features left in Finnish politics. One was the exclusion of the Conservative Party from office when the other parties refused to co-operate with it; another was the conflict on farming issues between MTK, representing producers, and SAK, representing consumers.[2] These issues of conflict in Finnish politics

---

[1] Helander 1982, 184-185.

[2] Elder et al. 1982, 168-172. The interests of industrial workers, supported by SAK, and farmers, supported by the Confederation of Farmers and Forestry Owners (MTK), were

are no longer as relevant as they were in the early 1980s, and Finland in the 1990s significantly differs from previous decades. It is not an overstatement to say that there is a new Finland in a new Europe, based on the following:

1. The Soviet Union has collapsed and communism no longer exists as a credible political force. Communist attitudes had already begun to change in the mid 1980s, when Gorbachev became the new Soviet leader and introduced more openness. The final breaking point came in 1989 with the fall of the Berlin wall, which led to the collapse of the communist regimes in Eastern Europe during 1990. The cold-war era is consequently over and the EU is expanding eastwards. At a referendum in 1994, Finnish voters supported a Finnish application for membership in the EU. The application was approved by the EU member states and Finland joined in 1995, the same time as Austria and Sweden. Estonia, Hungary, Poland and the Czech Republic are the first former communist countries to seek membership in the EU early in the twenty-first century. In 1999, Finland also became a member of the European Monetary Union (EMU), which includes a gradual introduction of the single European currency in 1999-2002.
2. After the Second World War, domestic coalition building in Finland was affected not only by internal political and ideological cleavages, but also by Finland's distinctive relationship with the Soviet Union. The so-called night-frost crisis in 1958, and the note-crisis in 1961, were the most serious incidents where the influence of the Soviet Union over Finnish domestic politics became obvious.[1] As noted in

often diametrically opposed in the 1950s, which inevitably led to conflict between the left-wing parties and the Agrarian Party. Red-Green coalitions were as frequent as they were short-lived. In addition, the Agrarian candidate U. Kekkonen narrowly won the Presidential election over his Social Democratic opponent in 1956, causing a great deal of antagonism among Social Democratic leaders towards Kekkonen's strong connection to the Kremlin. (Arter 1987, 167) Two weeks after Kekkonen became President the most serious conflict of the century on income policy occurred when SAK, led by Social Democrats, started a general strike in order to obtain compensation for price increases. The strike lasted three weeks.

[1] The main reason for the 'night-frost' crisis was Kremlin's disapproval of SDP's appointment as chairman the pro-Western veteran politician V. Tanner, who in 1946 had been committed to prison on charges of war crimes and had for a long time openly warned against Soviet expansionism. (Arter 1981, 223) A coalition government, formed in 1958, included two supporters of the new Social Democratic chairman, the right-wing

point 1, the communist ideology no longer exists as a political force and former communists have formed the Left Wing Alliance. Ideological cleavages among the left-wing parties have therefore withered away, and after the Finlandised years of press self-censorship a freer political debate has emerged in Finnish domestic politics.[1] The Conservatives became an acceptable coalition partner after the 1987 parliamentary election, and boasted the prime minister post 1987-91. After 1983, governments have also functioned without resignations for their whole terms of office (four years), whilst governments during the 1940-70s were as frequent as they were short-lived. A diminishing farming population has furthermore led to less intense conflict on producer vs. consumer interests. The political climate has therefore changed, with the strong polarisation between political parties becoming barely perceptible. The best evidence of the new climate is that all political parties have, in the 1990s, gained effective access to governments, including the Greens. The last two governments have

---

Conservative Party, the Agrarian Party, the Swedish Speaking Party and the Liberals. The Kremlin was not pleased with the coalition government, where both the Conservatives and the 'Tannerites' took part. As a result trade negotiations with the Soviet Union were suspended. The Agrarians, who had good contacts with the Kremlin, left the government, which subsequently had to resign. The following government appointed in 1959 was led by the Agrarians and the 'night frost' crisis was over. (Arter 1987, 177-178) The so-called 'note-crisis' occured in 1961, when the Kremlin handed a Note to the Finnish ambassador in Moscow. The Kremlin was concerned about a renewed German militarism in Europe, and the political instability in Finland. In the Note, the Soviet Union proposed joint military talks in accordance with article two of the Treaty, which would clearly have undermined Finland's aspirations to neutrality. In later meetings between the Finnish and Soviet foreign ministers, it also became clear that the Kremlin was anxious about the upcoming Finnish presidential election in 1962. The Social Democrats did not support the president in office, who had a strong support in the Kremlin, but instead appointed their own candidate, together with the Conservatives. The crisis was solved by top-level negotiations and the abandonment of the Social Democratic and Conservative presidential candidate. Opponents to Kekkonen regarded the Note as merely a strategic measure by him to secure a second period in office, which he eventually did. No evidence has emerged on whether the Note was ordered by Kekkonen or not. Suspicions have nonetheless remained unanswered. Relations were normalised when the Kremlin was assured by the president in office that Finland's lenient policy towards the Soviet Union remained unaltered. (Arter 1987, 182-185.)

[1] Salminen 1996.

been labelled Rainbow coalitions with only the Centre Party, Christian League and Progressive Party left in opposition.[1]

Table 1.2 Support for political parties in parliamentary elections 1987-99 (percentage of votes cast)

Party	1987	1991	1995	1999
Social Democratic Party	24.1	22.1	28.3	22.9
Centre Party	17.6	24.8	19.8	22.4
Conservative Party	23.1	19.3	17.9	21.0
Left Wing Alliance	13.6	10.1	11.2	10.9
Swedish People's Party	5.3	5.5	5.5	5.1
Christian League	2.6	3.0	3.0	4.2
Rural Party	6.3	4.8	1.3	1.0
Green League	4.0	6.8	6.5	7.3
Progressive Party	-	-	2.7	1.0
Others	3.3	3.5	0.9	4.2

Source: Official Statistics of Finland

3. The relationship between the parliament, government and president has changed with the abolition of the antiquated rules on qualified majorities in parliament for most economic legislation. This has meant a move to a more West-European style of parliamentary democracy. Until 1992, the minimum-winning coalition in Finland was not the normal 50 per cent 'plus one' but 66 per cent 'plus one'. One third of the members of parliament could thus veto any legislative proposal, which then was to be left in abeyance until after the next parliamentary election. Important economic legislation demanded a five-sixth majority in parliament to be declared urgent, which was required for an

[1] Of a total of 66 governments since Finland gained independence from Russia in 1917, only six have been short-lived minority governments. They have most often been red-green coalitions between Social Democrats and Agrarians, including some of the minor parties. The four largest parties (Social Democrats, Conservatives, Agrarians, and Communists) have never all at once taken part in coalition governments. Up to 1944 and between 1948 and 1966 the Communists were excluded. The Conservatives took part only sporadically in 1958, 1962, and 1964 but have without interruption taken part from 1987 onwards. In the 1960-80s it was mainly coalitions between the Social Democrats, Centre Party and Communists.

enactment during the same parliament. Such legislation also required a two-thirds majority to be passed in the third reading. Constitutional amendments also demanded a five-sixth majority of the votes. Before 1992 the president could, without formalised consultation, dissolve the parliament and order new elections. After the constitutional amendment in 1992, this can only be made on the proposal by the prime minister, provided that both the parliamentary party groups, and the speaker of parliament have been consulted. All parliament acts still have to be ratified by the president. If he or she refuses, the handling of the law returns to the parliament, but if the parliament again approves the bill, it comes into force without the president's approval. If the president refused to ratify an act before 1992, it could not be handled by the parliament again until after the next parliamentary election. The parliament has therefore (formally) increased in importance in the 1990s at the cost of the president's power.

4. The established quasi corporatist arrangements, i.e. negotiations on a tripartite or bipartite basis, have continuously been taking place Finland, and the broad-based incomes policy system has proved to be remarkably durable. The latest was agreed in 1997 and was in force between 1.1.1998-31.12.1999.[1] The main economic interest groups therefore still play a significant role in Finnish policy making. After five years of continuous broad-based settlements some influential trade unions, like the Paperworker's and Transport Union, did not agree to any broad-based settlement for 2000-02, despite the fact that the main economic interest groups and the government heavily supported a new settlement. The reason for the reluctancy of these unions was that they sought after higher wage increases than a settlement would have allowed for. Previously, only in 1973, 1977-78, 1980, 1983, 1994-95 have no settlements been made. Despite the importance of the main economic interest groups, it is, according to interviews with trade union representatives, no longer the case in Finland that the main economic interest groups more or less dictate the whole national economic and labour market agenda, as at the beginning of the 1970s.

[1] Negotiations on tri- and bipartite bases have not only been taking place in Finland, but also in countries like Ireland, Spain, Portugal, Belgium, the Netherlands, and Switzerland (Schmitter and Grote 1997). In Austria, corporatist arrangements have even been regarded in terms of an institutional dinosaur, unable to adapt to new environments. (Crepaz 1995.)

Based on the political events in Finland after the Second World War, it is relevant to state that Finnish politics was conflictual in character. Equally, it seems relevant to state that politics during the 1990s has become more consensual in character. Consensus can be defined as a form of government by deliberation, aiming to arrive at a rationally motivated decision where reasons persuasive to all are sought.[1] The concept of consensus is multifarious, however, and further qualifications are necessary. If using the term as categorising democratic systems, at least three different levels can be pointed out: basic, procedural and policy consensus. The first level, or basic consensus, is concerned with value beliefs and common goals in society, whilst the second level is concerned with a consensus over how conflicts are to be resolved.[2] All citizens do not, of course, have to believe in the same values and goals, and, for example, the presence of anti-system parties and alienated sub-groups, have been regarded as factors that would point to a non-consensual democracy.[3] Thus, the Rainbow coalition governments, the virtual absence of ideological polarisation between the political parties, the less intense conflict between producer and consumer interests and the continuous broad-based incomes policy settlements can all be regarded as examples of a basic consensus over common goals in Finland. Before the mid-1960s, the opposite was often the case with short-lived governments, strong ideological polarisation between political parties and conflicts between consumer and producer interests. There are also factors that point to the fact that there has been a consensus in Finland on rules on how conflicts are to be resolved (procedural consensus). The abolition of the qualified majority rules, the increase in parliamentary power at the cost of the president and the labour market rules agreed in broad based incomes policy settlements are examples of such a procedural consensus. There has in other words been agreement on the rules for disagreeing. Finland in the 1990s therefore largely complies with these two levels of consensual democracy. They are, however, only concerned with the overall political structures in society, and it would be foolhardy to bluntly characterise Finland as a consensual democracy, without an analysis of how issues of conflict have been resolved.

It is the third level, therefore, which can be regarded as policy consensus, that is the main point of reference of consensus in this thesis. If

---

[1] Sartori 1987, 91; Cohen 1989, 23.

[2] Sartori 1987, 90.

[3] Elder et al. 1983, 10.

the first two levels of consensual democracy are secured, it is at the third level where dissent, dissensus and opposition emerge.[1] Dissent, dissensus and opposition have not in any way been absent in Finnish labour market policy making in the 1990s. An ad hoc committee, with representatives of the main economic interest groups, was appointed in 1992, with the task of making the preparatory work for a government bill on a revised annual holiday act. The committee finished its work in 1993. The outcome of the committee's work was three different proposals due to disagreement between the participating representatives of the main economic interest groups. The first proposal was supported by the (independent) chairperson and some of the employers' representatives; the second was supported by a majority of the employers' representatives; and the third was supported by the workers' representatives. This issue has not been resolved and is currently not on the agenda. A second issue has been the development of negotiation mechanisms for the labour market, i.e. how to develop the opportunities for making more firm level and flexible agreements between individual employers and employees. This issue was equally difficult to resolve. An ad hoc committee was again appointed with the same representative basis as the previous ones. The result of this committee was, again, total disagreement between the parties and no new legislative statements on this issue.[2]

A more recent issue in the 1990s has been a revision of the employment contracts act. The most controversial statement in this act requires that individual conditions at work places, which are mentioned in the collective agreements, are automatically binding on all employment relationships. This basically means that the same terms and regulations workers have who are covered by collective agreements through their membership in trade unions shall also be applied to unorganised workers. Unorganised employers must also implement the collective agreement that covers his workers, even if the employer himself is not covered by any collective agreement.[3] This is known as the principle of universal commitment *(Yleissitovuus)*. A committee was appointed with the task of developing this act in 1995, on the same representative basis as the previous ones. It was to publish its result by the end of October 1997, but the committee was unable to meet its deadlines. The final deadline was set for 31.1.2000. In order to meet this deadline, the committee had to vote on

[1] Sartori 1987, 91.

[2] Bobacka 1996.

[3] Bruun et al. 1992, 35.

several of the outstanding issues where no agreement between the parties had been reached. The most conflictual issue was the one on who are to be bound by the principle of universal commitment. The Conservative Party and the employers' representatives in the committee heavily objected to an extension of the universal commitment, while the workers' representatives and the Social Democratic Party worked for an extension. The central confederations of trade unions and employers' associations were nonetheless able to reach a compromise on the issue at the final moment, which, according to SAK, was an acceptable solution. The Federation of Finnish Enterprises (SY), supported by the Conservative Party did not agree to the compromise, however, and there were even talks about a government crisis caused by this issue.[1] SAK was highly critical towards SY and stated that the organisation had not yet shown the maturity that is required from an organisation taking part in corporatist arrangements.[2] The committee's proposal is not yet finalised to become a government bill, however, and further negotiations are required on the explanatory notes for the act, i.e. how the act is to be interpreted.

There are also labour market issues that have been more successfully resolved. The most notable has been the introduction of a so-called buffer fund and the revision of the working hours act. The buffer fund was agreed on after the introduction of the EMU, in order to create a buffer against periods of economic recession. The establishment of the fund was decided in negotiations between the government and the main economic interest groups.[3] This thesis represents an issue, i.e. the revision of the working hours legislation, that also eventually was resolved, and where a final decision was made by parliament in 1996. It therefore also represents a case study of what from the outset seems to be successful consensus building. The case should also tell something about how dissent, dissensus and opposition has been dealt with in Finland in the 1990s, a Finland that fulfils many of the other characteristics of a consensual democracy. This book will consequently examine the relationship between organised

---

[1] Hufvudstadsbladet 9.2.2000.

[2] SAK public statement.

[3] The funds consist of two parts: an unemployment security, and a pension security. During prosperous years, higher social security and pension fees are collected from both employers and employees and, consequently, during recession periods a lower social security fee is collected, which is used against the balance of the previously collected funds. It is expected that the funds will be fully operative in four to six years time. In the future, the main economic interest groups will agree in annual negotiations about whether or not to increase the capital that is to be allocated to the funds. (Helsingin Sanomat 18.11.1997, A7.)

interests and the state in depth, seeking to answer the following question: *what does a sectoral analysis of working hours legislation tell us about labour market policy making in Finland in the 1990s?* The outline of the book follows a traditional way of analysing decision making processes, i.e. contextualisation, formulation, deliberation and implementation. It does not follow any specific methodology, but is eclectic in its approach to available empirical material.

2 Corporatism and Consensus Building

A common, and durable, theory that has focused on the structural relationships between organised interests and the state, has been corporatism. In 1997, Schmitter and Grote made an evaluation of what they called the persistent corporatist features of European politics. Bipartite and tripartite negotiations between organised interests and governments were still common in countries like Ireland, Spain, Portugal, Belgium, the Netherlands, Austria and Switzerland.[1] As noted in the introduction, in Austria, another study of corporatist arrangements even regarded them in terms of an institutional dinosaur, unable to adapt to new environments.[2] In Finland, two consecutive broad-based incomes policy settlements were concluded in 1995 and 1997. This also indicated that some form of corporatism was still a relevant political concept, explaining the relationship between the state and organised interests. The first aim of this chapter is consequently to evaluate corporatism as a theory explaining the structural relationship between states and organised interests.

The first problem arising from an evaluation of corporatism as concept is how to structure the vast amount of literature on the subject. From a historical perspective, three different meanings have been used: medieval, industrial and fascist corporatism. In the medieval period, corporatism was associated with a political culture that rested on authority, when hierarchical status was granted by state authorities to different estates and guilds. During the age of industrialism, from the mid nineteenth century onwards, corporatism was associated with a reaction against a developing social injustice, seen as a result of liberal capitalism. Corporatism did not oppose private property or work for class conflict, as did the emerging socialist theorists, but instead advocated a consensual, collectivist and hierarchical society based on the moral philosophy of Catholicism. The

---

[1] Schmitter and Grote 1997.

[2] Crepaz 1995.

third, fascist, form of corporatism is related to the emergence of an authoritarian regime in Italy in the 1920s. A corporatist system was installed, where the leadership of trade unions and employers' associations had to be appointed by the state, consequently enabling it to control the labour market and the economy. The system became an efficient means of subordinating labour directly under state control.[1] After the second world war a fourth variant of corporatism developed, attempting to explain the relationship between organised interests and the state. This variant was labelled *neo*corporatism (or new) in order to make the distinction from its predecessing variants. This chapter focuses on the fourth variant of corporatism from the post second world war period. For convenience, the term corporatism will be used throughout.[2]

A simple approach when analysing corporatism, is to evaluate it simply in *theoretical* and *descriptive* terms.[3] Theoretical corporatism is concerned with assumptions about the relationship between states and organised interests. Descriptive corporatism denotes empirically based evaluations of this relationship. This distinction provides a more comprehensive picture than chronological categorisations. Chronologically, authors of the first generation in the mid to late 1970s, developed corporatism as a political theory. A second generation, active in the early 1980s, treated the concept more in terms of empirical considerations. A third generation in the mid-1980s developed different levels of corporatism.[4] Such a distinction neither takes into account the initial early writings from the 1950s and 1960s, nor more recent writings from the 1990s. The theoretical-descriptive distinction also reflects another common categorisation that has been made, with a division between state corporatism, corporatism as interest intermediation and corporatism as an economic system.[5]

While corporatism is concerned with structural relationships between organised interests and the state, the most interesting, and least discussed, aspect of corporatism has been its normative foundation. Corporatism has

---

[1] Williamson 1989, 23-36.

[2] Both the concepts of corporatism and corporativism have been used in Scandinavia. In the Swedish language, corporativism was often used in order to make a clear distinction between the previous fascist forms of corporatism and the use of corporatist arrangements in the building of the Swedish welfare state.

[3] Williamson 1989, 67.

[4] Williamson 1989, 14-17.

[5] Cawson 1986, 22; Smith 1993, 29-32.

been normatively justified as a form of consensual politics, a feature also present in a pluralist theory. In a pluralist context

> ... consensus emerges from the play of interests in the marketplace game of politics; in [corporatism] consensus emerges from the self-subordination of special interests to a commonly developed conception of the public interest, enforced by the state.[1]

The second aim of this chapter is consequently to focus on *Consensus building in practice.*

Theoretical Corporatism

Philippe Schmitter has usually been cited as the one who began the discussion on corporatism as theory in the 1970s. No one contests his view about the growing importance of organised interests. His argument was that the organised interests could not all be characterised in the same way, but were to be regarded as differing according to various dimensions.[2] Such dimensions were, for example, the degree of voluntarism and overlap in membership, the success of organised interests in exercising their representational function, the importance of recognition by the state, the control of leadership selection by state regimes etc. These differences could, according to Schmitter, be clustered into specific ideal-type configurations of relationships between the state and interest organisations.[3] Corporatism was regarded as a concept, which denoted these features of modern interest group intermediation. Schmitter subsequently contrasted corporatism with pluralist views of politics.

The Corporatist-Pluralist Debate

Pluralist views of organised interests could, according to Schmitter, be defined as systems of interest intermediation, where interests in society were organised into multiple, voluntary, competitive, non-hierarchically ordered categories that had no monopoly of representation over their respective categories. The state did not control the election of leadership to

---

[1] Garson 1978, 47.

[2] Schmitter 1974, 96.

[3] Schmitter 1979, 63-65.

these units, nor license, recognise or create them in any sense. The opposite to such a pluralist view of politics, that is corporatism, was

> ... a system of interest-representation in which the constituent units are organised into a limited number of singular, compulsory, non-competitive, hierarchically ordered and functionally differentiated categories, recognised or licensed (if not created) by the state, and granted a deliberate representational monopoly within their respective categories, in exchange for observing certain control on their selection of leaders and articulation of demands and supports.[1]

It was a political process, where large organisations that had a monopoly over specific interests in society, engaged with state agencies in the implementation of public policy.[2] The role of interest groups became both regulatory and representative. Their regulatory function included an implementation of public policy decisions, while their representative function was, at the same time, to gain acceptance from their members on the agreed policy decisions.[3]

The aim of a corporatist theory was, according to Schmitter, to show the inadequacy of pluralist and Neo-Marxist views of politics and develop a kind of synthesis between them. In other words, he presented a new theory for explaining the relationship between organised interests and the state. Pluralist approaches were, according to corporatists, inappropriate, since they were seen as based on underlying assumptions of a competitive political marketplace with multiple centres of power. They were also regarded as based on a methodological individualism, where collective interests were seen as an aggregation of individual interests, as well as a neutral state, which was disengaged from interest conflicts.[4] The theory of corporatism contested this view, basing its assumptions on a non-competitive political marketplace, where the relationship between the state and interest organisations was not as easily separable as the pluralist theory would have suggested. Corporatism was also contrasted with Neo-Marxism, which was regarded as leaning too heavily on the assumption of political interests based on economic class relationships, where the role of the state was seen as merely an instrument of a dominant class or as an arena for class conflict. The state was in the Neo-Marxist view seen as non-

[1] Schmitter 1974, 94.

[2] Cawson 1986, 38.

[3] Smith 1993, 31.

[4] Cawson 1985, 2.

autonomous.[1] While the basic concept of interest according to pluralism was individual preferences, Neo-Marxism concentrated on class-consciousness. Corporatism was seen as combining both perspectives. Organisations were to be treated as collective actors, aggregated from their members' individual interests. Individual interests shaped the nature of organised interests, but at the same time the organised interests were also seen as to some extent controlling the individual interests.[2] It was a two-way relationship between individual and organisational interests.

The problem with contrasting corporatism and pluralism soon became obvious. The corporatist interpretation of pluralism was seen by many authors as superficial when they could not see much difference between pluralism (especially variants such as corporate pluralism), and the more liberal forms of corporatism.[3] (Liberal corporatism was seen as an alternative to the pre-industrial and authoritarian forms of corporatism where the state had been able to control the organised interests. It featured a voluntary integration of conflicting social groups in the shaping of economic policy. It was based on consensus building at the top or elite levels where the leaders of large interest organisations had a great deal of autonomy in their dealings with the state.[4]) Schmitter's starting point of making a distinction between corporatism and a very basic definition of pluralism was therefore heavily criticised. According to his definition of pluralism, all interests in society were supposed to have access to, and could make themselves heard, at some stage of decision making processes. Authors who objected to Schmitter's views of pluralism noted instead that there were alternative lines of arguments in the pluralist literature. For example, pluralism had also been regarded in terms of regularised relations, as well as open conflict and ad hoc competition.[5] In 1964, Lowi argued that pluralist decision making structures could vary according to the subject matter of the issue. He used the term regulatory politics, where government decisions favoured one party, while others were disfavoured. Distributive politics were seen as the opposite form, where some parties were favoured without any disfavour for others.[6] In a pluralist context, the resources of an interest group could furthermore vary according to the social position of the

[1] Cawson 1985, 2-3.

[2] Cawson 1985, 4, Offe 1981, 123.

[3] Martin 1983, 96; Jordan 1984, 142ff.

[4] Lehmbruch 1979, 54.

[5] Jordan 1984, 142-143.

[6] Lowi 1964.

group, the way it was organised, the skill of its leadership, the size of the group and the degree of mobilisation. The organisational resources were therefore limited and unequally distributed, meaning that interest groups had different opportunities for influencing public policies.[1] The concept of iron-triangles, for example, represented stable and regularised relations in the United States between specific organised interests, the federal administration, and congressional committees. These relations were also segmented into different policy areas.[2]

If the crucial point for a theory to become accepted is whether it better explains political behaviour than other alternative theories, then corporatism was not a good alternative to pluralism.[3] The pluralist-corporatist debate became largely an exercise of words over what corporatism and pluralism were, and what they were not. The problem with the corporatist - pluralist distinction was that the concept of pluralism had been developed over many years with different meanings added. The problem for authors on corporatism was that they tried to provide an alternative to a field of research that had for a long time been 'occupied' by pluralism. Pluralism had become a constantly moving target, which was easy to defend, and hard to attack when pluralists had no problem in finding aspects of pluralist theory that resembled the corporatist theory.[4] If the concept of iron-triangles, for example, had been developed in a non-pluralist context, it would have resembled corporatism more than pluralism. The corporatist theorists would therefore have been better off not contrasting it to pluralism, but instead developed a new theory of the state/interest relationship.[5] The unfruitful debate between authors advocating corporatism, and authors presenting different pluralist views of politics, did not mean, however, that the basic components of corporatism were inaccurate or uninteresting. The only problem was that corporatism was no new theory explaining relationships between organised interests and states as Schmitter and his supporters suggested.

One area where this was clearly visible was the notion of power. Pluralists had a clearly defined, albeit simplistic, view of power in society. According to classical pluralism, power was an observable phenomenon that was dispersed in liberal democracies. According to a neo-pluralist

---

[1] Dahl 1961, 228.

[2] Jordan 1981.

[3] Williamson 1989, 4.

[4] Grant 1985, 117.

[5] Jordan 1984, 145.

view, power had become unobservable, structural and ideological and was concentrated in grand issues and dispersed in secondary issues.[1] Classical pluralist notions of power therefore involved a focus on behaviour in decision making, where observable conflicts of interests were seen as policy preferences revealed by political participation. The central questions in pluralist notions of power were who had gained access to the decision making processes, and who could be seen to influence outcomes.[2] Corporatism as theory had never developed any specific notion of power, but used the same views of power as did the pluralists, i.e. power revealed as participation.

The assumptions of regulatory politics, a non-competitive political marketplace and a non-independent state, represented in both corporatism and pluralism, nonetheless point to an important feature of relationships between organised interests and the state. If assuming that non-competitiveness is sometimes the case in some sectors, a view also supported by pluralists, then the interesting problem becomes the way in which an imperfect political marketplace functions. The assumption is that imperfect political marketplaces also imply imperfect reasoning where powerful (and resourceful) participants do not always have to use rational arguments to get their views accepted. If they cannot find any appropriate arguments to support their standpoints, they can instead simply use their resources to get their views accepted. From this it follows that '... rational arguments are one of the few forms of power the powerless still possess'.[3] This approach naturally demands a focus on decision making practices, since a focus on structural arrangements does not provide much assistance in evaluations of actual decision making. Many authors also concluded their arguments (where they should have started), by stating that more in-depth research on corporatism was needed in order to gain more accurate knowledge of the influence of interest organisations.[4] There was, however, more to a corporatist theory than merely a clash with pluralism. Unfortunately, much of corporatist theorising was also characterised by inadequacies, and often reiterated arguments already established in pluralist theory.

---

[1] Smith 1993, 210.

[2] Lukes 1974, 12.

[3] Flyvbjerg 1998, 229.

[4] Heisler 1979, 286; Helander 1983, 42; Cawson 1986, 36; Eriksen 1990, 348; Jordan and Schubert 1992, 26; Lewin 1994, 66.

Corporatism and the State

A major problem in corporatist theorising became how to define the role of the state in relation to interest organisations. Pahl and Winkler argued that in a *state* corporatist system, the state controlled all economic policy making. The interests of the state as a whole consequently came before narrow sectoral demands by, for example, individual companies or branches on the labour market. The essence of state corporatism was private ownership but state control.[1] In a corporatist state, representation was mediated through a system of corporations, and state intervention occurred through these same corporations. In pure parliamentary systems, on the other hand, representation was secured through voting and intervention occurred through legislation.[2] Representation and intervention became institutionally fused in state corporatist systems, when interest organisations became involved in policy-making processes. They were subsequently supposed to merge with the state.

A theory of corporatism as state form received much criticism. The main point was that corporatist theorists never defined the state. A logical definition of the state would have seemed to be governments, since corporatist theorists were usually concerned with relations between governments and interest organisations.[3] Authors rejecting corporatism as a state form regarded the state as becoming weakened and manipulated when it would only execute solutions made by the interest organisations, who were seen as dominating the policy process.[4] The interest organisations were therefore not merging with the state, but the state became captured by the organised interests. It was furthermore argued that the state could not be seen as constituting a single institution, but that it varied greatly between different policy areas. While state corporatism could be valid in one area, other forms of corporatism could be more relevant in another.[5] This line of argument conversed with the pluralist notion of interest groups and the state. According to pluralist views of politics, there were multiple centres of power in society, none of which were wholly sovereign. Truman furthermore acknowledged, that institutionalised relationships between

---

[1] Pahl and Winkler 1977.

[2] Jessop 1990, 120; Cox 1981, 82-83.

[3] Martin 1983, 87.

[4] Nedelmann and Meier 1977, 48, 57.

[5] Nedelmann and Meier 1979, 104-105; Martin 1983, 99.

departments or agencies could develop, leading to other interests being ignored.[1]

If developing a theory of relationships between organised interests and states, one has to assume that it was to be seen as a general theory. As it was, no general theory was accepted as such, but corporatism became a theory of specific forms of interest intermediation. The problem corporatist theorists faced, was that the distinctiveness to pluralism was irrelevant, since theoretical assumptions of corporatism had already been covered in pluralist theories. Advocates of corporatism consequently realised the deficiency of pure forms of state corporatism, and soon started to develop more intricate and limited forms.[2] *Societal* corporatism was introduced as an alternative to state corporatism. This form of corporatism was present in political systems characterised by multilayered territorial units, open competitive electoral processes and open party-systems, as well as ideologically varied executive authorities. State corporatism, on the other hand, was regarded as present in political systems characterised by territorial sub-units strongly tied to central bureaucracies, non-existent elections, a party system monopolised by a single party and ideologically exclusive authorities. State corporatism was regarded in terms of the authoritarian state form of corporatism while societal corporatism was regarded in terms of an advanced, capitalist and democratic welfare state.[3] *Liberal* corporatism also, as already noted, provided an alternative to the authoritarian and pre-industrial forms of corporatism. The introduction of societal and liberal corporatism meant that a corporatist distinctiveness was significantly reduced where these features resembled areas of pluralist discussion. Pluralism could also be seen as signified by assumptions of multilayered territorial units, open competitive electoral processes, open party-systems and ideologically varied executive authorities.

In Scandinavia, the relationship between organised interests and states was supposed to be highly corporatist in character. Sweden was the best example in representing a single model, defined as an archetype of *Social Democratic* corporatism where the Social Democratic Party and the largest confederation of trade unions (LO) co-operated closely in developing the Swedish welfare model.[4] Corporatism as an overall concept was more or less taken for granted since many studies in Sweden had pointed to

---

[1] Truman 1951, 10.

[2] Schmitter 1974, 92; Cawson 1978; 1986.

[3] Schmitter 1974, 103, 105.

[4] Lewin 1994, 59.

regularised forms of relationships between organised interests and the state.[1] Authors during the 1980-90s became concerned with whether it was the state, or organised interests that were the main independent variables in explaining the strong form of corporatism in Sweden. One interpretation of corporatism was that organised interests had superseded the role of parliament when a small number of influential individuals from political parties, organisations, media and public administration had formed groups that dominated specific issues. The state and interest organisations worked closely together, and the state's ambition had been to incorporate organised interests into more and more policy areas; the state was supposed to have lost its autonomy and authority. Rothstein's (1988) thesis was that corporatist arrangements in Sweden could be seen as a specific Social Democratic institutionalisation of class conflict, resulting from working class organisational strength.[2] He argued that the main independent variable in explaining the occurrence of weak or strong corporatist systems, had been the function and character of the state. The Swedish state was centralised, but not closed, bureaucratic but not authoritarian, and differentiated, but not without central co-ordination of policy. This had enabled the development of a strong corporatist system in Sweden.[3]

Rothstein's description of Sweden also to some extent correlated with the types II and III of Nordlinger's (1981) categorisations of state autonomy. Nordlinger made a typology of four kinds of explanations for the authoritative actions of democratic states. The typology was based on fundamental distinctions between whether the action by the state was coincident, or non-coincident with the preferences of the public. Type I of his typology referred to cases where the state and societal preferences were divergent, but the authoritative action was non-coincident with the state preferences, the state was non-autonomous.[4] Type II of his typology referred to cases, where the state and societal preferences were divergent, but the authoritative decisions coincided with the preferences of the state. The state was consequently autonomous. Type III depicted cases where state-society preferences were at first divergent, but public officials purposefully brought about changes in the societal preferences, to make them more in line with the state's preferences. Type IV was cases where the state and societal preferences did not diverge, and the authoritative

---

1 Heckscher 1946; Elvander 1969; Rothstein 1988, 1992.

2 Rothstein 1988, 239-254.

3 Rothstein 1991, 168-169.

4 Nordlinger 1981, 27-28.

actions were coincident with the state preferences.[1] The problem is that although the state action may coincide with the preferences of the main economic interest groups, it does not necessarily mean that they coincide with the societal preferences. Although Nordlinger's typology may provide a valuable tool for determining state autonomy in pluralist societies, it becomes rather limited in a corporate pluralist context.

It is of vital importance to notice that Rothstein argued in a Swedish context. Sweden was depicted as a unique country from a corporatist perspective because the powerful Social Democratic Party had for a long time led governments and developed the Swedish welfare model. Possibilities for generalisations were therefore restricted. It was, for example, not applicable to a Finnish context of a politically divided labour movement during the post-war decades. The counterargument to the non-autonomous state was that corporatist channels of influence could in fact strengthen the state. Common goals were achieved more efficiently when organised interests became responsible for both popular and unpopular regulations. It was a positive-sum game, where both the interest organisations and the state benefited; interest organisations had a direct voice in public policy, and the state could delegate some responsibility to them.[2] However, such general characteristics can also be discussed in a pluralist framework.

The distinctiveness of corporatism in terms of a limited number of non-competitive, hierarchically ordered and functionally differentiated organisations that had received a representational monopoly in their dealings with the state, was greatly reduced since the same themes had been discussed in a pluralist context.[3] The more intricate and limited forms of corporatism became even more reminiscent of the pluralist discussion. As a result, the essence of corporatism as theory became barely distinguishable from different variants of pluralism. The merits of the corporatism – pluralism debate consequently lay more in empirical discussions where Heckscher's evaluations of the Swedish system in terms of free corporatism, Rokkan's evaluation of Norwegian politics in terms of corporate pluralism and Heisler and Kvavik's evaluations of a European co-optive polity were the most notable.[4] More recent empirical studies of

---

[1] Nordlinger 1981, 28-29.

[2] Eriksen 1990, 348.

[3] Truman 1951; Lowi 1964.

[4] Heckscher 1946; Rokkan 1966, Heisler and Kvavik 1974.

state-interest organisational relationships further verified the extent to which corporatism as a concept was fragmented.

Descriptive Corporatism

Authors focusing on relationships between the state and organised interests adopted the corporatist concept in their empirical analyses, and in many cases added their own prefixes. This was not totally inappropriate, since there were clear indications that the functioning of organised interests in Europe differed from its American counterpart. Different categories of authors implementing corporatism can be pointed out. Political scientists mainly regarded corporatism as interest intermediation between organised interests and governments, with a focus on *participation* in policy making. Political economists mainly regarded corporatism as an economic system and as an explanatory factor in explaining economic performance. Both these categories largely focused on comparative analyses of corporatism between countries.

Heckscher (1946) had already described the Swedish system of intense collaboration between organised interests and governments after the Second World War, in terms of *free* corporatism.[1] He noted that interest organisations in Sweden had extensive opportunities for influencing political parties, since voting behaviour was supposed to be largely influenced by the appearance of candidates belonging to an interest organisation. The parties therefore usually selected candidates with important group attachments for the party list. (The voters in Sweden voted for party lists and not for individual candidates.[2]) The organisations could also influence politics through their participation in royal commissions. These commissions dealt with all important issues, which were brought before parliament. The organisations had furthermore gained access to the legislative process through the so-called remiss-system, where they could comment on public policy issues before the final decision in parliament. These forms of participation were seen as far more important than traditional interest organisational pressure activities in forms of lobbying. Lobbying was regarded as unnecessary in Sweden as there were vast opportunities for open participation.[3]

---

[1] Heckscher 1946.

[2] Heckscher 1958, 164.

[3] Heckscher 1958, 165-168.

In Norway, Rokkan's research denoted a specific and close relationship between the state and organised interests, characterised as *corporate pluralism*. The political situation in Norway after the Second World War was that the socialist and non-socialist parties were almost tied electorally. The voting majority of the socialist parties in parliament between 1945 and 1961 was highest in 1945 with 52.9 per cent, and lowest in 1949 with 51.5 per cent. The governing Labour Party adopted a strategy, which was to try and keep the influence of the radical left-wing splinter movement to a minimum, and thereby attract the votes of the masses halfway between the poles of the political system. This obviously led to a drift of politics to the political centre when the large parties agreed on a wide range of domestic policy issues.[1] From a functional-economic dimension, Rokkan developed a simplified three-pole model where the corners consisted of labour, farmers and business. The battle for votes did not take place at the political extremes, but at the halfway range between the poles. For example, the struggle for the votes of the new middle class was between the poles of labour and business, votes of the rural middle class between the poles of business and farmers and votes of marginal smallholders and fishermen between the poles of farmers and labour.[2] In political conflicts between the poles, the result was that no political group could rely solely on their electoral strength, because organisational resources had become increasingly important. This also led to the dual channels of influence in public decision making, famously stated as, 'votes count but resources decide'. Rokkan thus shifted focus from electoral politics to pressure group politics. It is important to note that corporate pluralism was no new theory but more a description of interest representation in Norway.[3] By using the concept of corporate pluralism, he recognised that corporatism was a variant of pluralism and thus overcame many of the definitional dilemmas that later haunted the corporatist theorists in their search for a specific corporatist theory. Corporate pluralism was supposed to capture the complex, multifarious and ad hoc characteristic of Norwegian politics.[4] It drew heavily on Dahl's notions of pluralism where resourceful organised interests had better possibilities for influencing policy processes than less resourceful organised interests.

[1] Rokkan 1966, 90-91.

[2] Rokkan 1966, 92-93.

[3] Jordan 1984, 147.

[4] Heisler 1979, 284.

Other research in Norway nonetheless indicated that overall Norwegian politics was not corporatist in character, albeit that there were some corporatist traits of an integration of interest representation in public policy making.[1] In Denmark, research on external involvement in law making also indicated that there was no significant overall picture of corporatist intermediation. The dominant pattern was that many different groups used several channels of access. Damgaard and Eliassen therefore regarded the Danish system as characterised by pluralist corporatism as opposed to societal corporatism.[2] Results in both Norway and Denmark summed up the basic problem with corporatism. It could not be seen as representing whole systems, but only some specific areas of interest intermediation. The value of corporatism as a general phenomenon was therefore greatly reduced.

From a comparative perspective Heisler and Kvavik developed a single model of policy making in Europe, which according to them could offer a strategy for comparative studies of smaller European countries. The common denominator for a European polity could be seen as one of co-optation, where interest groups had gained continuous and regularised access to the highest level of the political system. The authors' intention was to characterise a European type of political systems, including a set of variables that could be implemented.[3] They rejected the widely used Eastonian model of policy making where pressure groups were situated at the input-side of policy processes. A growing number of pressure groups, and a decline in ideological parties, had enabled the development of highly articulated pluralist structures, which represented political, social and economic cleavages. Western Europe had become characterised by a scheme of sectoral representation akin to corporatism or corporate pluralism. Heisler and Kvavik took as examples the Scandinavian practices where the committee system had provided interest groups with access to public decision making, and where the so-called remiss-system had enabled organised interests to comment on legislative proposals according to their respective areas of interest. The appointment of Economic and Social Councils in France, the Netherlands, Weimar Germany and Norway was seen as another example of the European co-optive model. The common denominator for European politics should consequently be characterised as

---

[1] Christensen and Egeberg 1979, 256.

[2] Damgaard and Eliassen 1978, 311-312.

[3] Heisler and Kvavik 1974, 37; Heisler 1979, 278.

a decision making structure, where the peak interest organisations had continuous and regular access to the decision making arenas.[1]

The intentions of Heisler and Kvavik were not to develop any new theory of pressure group politics or corporatism, but only to point to different factors that had to be taken into account when evaluating a European feature of making policy. Their main argument was that in order to understand political processes in Europe focus must be on the political processes themselves, rather than on the environmental factors that were supposed to influence politics.[2] Some years later, Heisler returned to this theme, and concluded that what was supposed to be a set of variables in order better to understand the complex picture of politics, had in many cases become viewed as the central explanatory variable.[3] Although there were signs of a common European co-optive polity, a single form of corporatism or corporatist like systems was difficult to find, hence the development of different corporatist sub-categories.

Empirical research by political scientists on corporatism mainly focused on interest representation in different governmental bodies and organs.[4] They focused on, for example, number of organisations, membership in organisations, interest organisational participation in committees and commissions, and their involvement in the remiss-system. (The remiss-system was more institutionalised in Norway and Sweden, than in Denmark and Finland, where it was not regarded as a particularly important feature of decision making.) The results of these analyses were that representatives of interests were granted access to decision making processes in their respective areas of interests. Research in Finland also focused to a high extent on corporatism as interest intermediation and participation.[5]

Descriptions of corporatism were further extended with the introduction of sub-categories. Sectoral and tripartite *Macro* corporatism focused on the relationship between national labour and business organisations and governments. Such macro-corporatist features enabled authors to distinguish between *strong, medium* and *weak* corporatist states. Austria, Norway, Sweden and the Netherlands were usually seen as representing strong corporatist states; Denmark, Finland, Germany,

---

[1] Heisler and Kvavik 1974, 38-65.

[2] Heisler and Kvavik 1974, 71.

[3] Heisler 1979, 278.

[4] Crouch and Dore 1990, 3.

[5] Huuska 1968, 1970; Helander 1982, 1983.

Belgium and Switzerland were seen as medium corporatist states; while the United States, Canada, France and Great Britain were considered weak corporatist states.[1] Sectoral *Meso* corporatism focused on interest organisations and their relationship to central departments or regional agencies at sectoral levels. *Micro* corporatism focused on direct negotiations between individual firms and state agencies.[2] In Scandinavia, *local* corporatism was introduced as a specific form of corporatist structures. It was regarded in terms of ad hoc contacts between local business executives, trade unionists and local public officials.[3] The analyses of micro and local corporatism were not totally appropriate, however. If shifting focus from corporatism at a national (macro) level, to corporatism at a local (micro) level, there was a risk that it became not a shift within corporatism, but a shift away from corporatism. All industrial relations at workplaces, or between local businesses where some public official was involved, were not necessarily corporatist in character. It was not at all necessary that public officials either were controlled by organised interests or themselves controlled what happened at the local level. It could be more a question of client and customer relationship.[4]

The concept of corporatism was not only implemented by political scientists, but also by political economists, who focused on corporatism as an independent variable. Their research was usually directed towards the economic policies of small states, indicating economic system where: 'the state directs and controls predominantly privately owned business according to four principles: unity, order, nationalism and success'.[5] In capitalist systems, production took place in free markets with marginal state interventionism. Capital remained in private hands and there was no nationalisation of enterprises. In corporatist systems, the state was enabled to overcome the conflicts in society, which enhanced the opportunities for the state to work for the interest of nations as a whole.[6] Political economists also focused on the political conditions for successful economic performance in a world economy characterised by uncertainty. These political conditions were defined in terms of both the basic political structure, as well as policy strategy.[7] Pekkarinen et al. introduced the

[1] Cawson 1986, 99; Schmitter 1982; Lehmbruch 1982; Schmidt 1982; Katzenstein 1985.

[2] Cawson 1986, 79.

[3] Hernes and Selvik 1979, 274.

[4] Cawson 1986, 120.

[5] Winkler 1976, 103.

[6] Cawson 1986, 22-23.

[7] Hicks 1988, 131.

concept of *social* corporatism. The concept was based on an economic system with centralised wage bargaining, as well as bargaining between the government and organised interests on economic and social policies. The main features of social corporatism were that all social groups on the labour market were included in the sharing of welfare benefits, and in sharing the burden of welfare adjustments.[1] Social corporatism was thus more or less an attempt to explain economic performance by broad-based national incomes policy settlements. *Democratic* corporatism was used by Katzenstein, implying an 'ideology of social partnership', where a large proportion of workers and producers were included in interest organisations. The relationship between these organisations was voluntary and informal, involving a continuous pluralist bargaining with bureaucracies and political parties.[2] He also focused on the extent to which social conditions, political institutions and public policies facilitated shifts in factors that influenced the economic efficiency of states. Such factors included state compensations for instabilities in the economy, an example of which is incomes policies.[3] The social and democratic versions of corporatism highly resembled the liberal corporatist view, which was based on voluntary integration of conflicting groups in economic policy making.

Corporatism as a theoretical concept was seen as too broad and simple to be fruitfully operationalised. Doubts were also raised as to whether corporatism really mattered in explaining economic performance.[4] After the introduction of broad-based income policy settlements in Finland it could not be proved that the settlements had any decisive impact on economic performance, although Uusitalo noted that there was no reason to underestimate the 'possibilities' for such an impact.[5]

The sub-categories of corporatism did not give any new theoretical insights, but were instead concerned with practical applications of corporatism. The problem was that although the empirical research focused on participation, one has to assume that the *aim* of the corporatist literature was to focus on the power and influence of interest organisations over public policies. In stressing the importance of interest groups in policy making, one is not only interested in participation, but also in what actually

[1] Katzenstein 1985, 105; Pekkarinen et al. 1992, 2-3.

[2] Katzenstein 1985, 32-33.

[3] Katzenstein 1985, 29, 48-50.

[4] Therborn 1987, 280.

[5] Uusitalo 1983, 24.

takes place when organised interests 'represent'.[1] According to much research done on corporatism, participation by interest organisations was often seen as equivalent to influence, when influence and participation are, of course, not synonymous. As a theory focusing on different structures of state-interest organisational relationships, corporatism consequently failed to provide any explanation of influence since influence requires an evaluation of both practical decision making and structural arrangements.

Summary

The most important question to be asked is what the merits of corporatism have been? The attempts to explain the relationship between states and organised interests according to a corporatist theory failed in the sense that the ground it was supposed to cover had already largely been dealt with in the pluralist literature. Schmitter's contrast between pluralism and corporatism consequently was unprofitable. (His assumptions nonetheless resulted in a vast amount of interest and research on the subject.) The main merits of discussions in this area, therefore lies in the early empirical evaluations of interest intermediation where Heckscher (1946) and Rokkan (1966) had provided new insights into the relationship between states and organised interests in Sweden and Norway.

Descriptive analyses of corporatism were regarded in terms of, for example, pluralist corporatist, social democratic, macro, strong, medium, weak, meso, micro or local corporatism. This indicated a lack of any deductive significance of corporatism as theory since it proved to be difficult to operationalise. All these different categorisations of the relationships between interests and governments were most probably accurate: the problem was that they had become extremely reductionist, and they had never provided any deeper picture of how this relationship worked in practice and the effects it had on modern democratic systems.

Although corporatism largely failed to provide a distinct theory of the relationship between states and organised interests, there are clearly visible features of regularised relationships where some (resourceful) organised interests have gained a regular voice in public policy making. In Finland this has taken place most notably through the broad-based incomes policy settlements and the participation of the main economic interest groups in different boards, commissions and committees. This relationship between

[1] Rothstein 1988, 242.

interest organisations and governments is still an important phenomenon in both Finland and many other Western European countries. The phenomenon can best be described in terms of *corporate pluralist* arrangements - without any reference to corporatism as a specific theory, but merely with reference to specific regulatory relationships between the state and organised interests, that was first indicated by Heckscher and Rokkan. *Corporate pluralism in a Finnish context is therefore defined as a system where the main economic interest groups listed in table 1 (except SY) have better possibilities to influence policy processes than other interest groups*. This influence has been possible through their participation in various boards, commissions and committees, as well as through the conclusion of broad based incomes policy settlements since 1968.

Normative Arguments on Corporate Pluralism and Consensus Building

It must be stressed that although an analysis of the development of new working hours legislation in Finland may be seen as relating to the corporatist debate, it does not follow that the analysis depends on the merit of any particular formulation of corporatism as theory. The analysis rests more on the basic essence of corporatism, which may be seen as a form of a close and regularised relationship between different interest groups and governments. Instead of trying to make a distinction between corporatism and pluralism, as Schmitter did, a more fruitful way would be to accept that there is no clear difference between the two concepts, and focus on a basic feature of the concepts where they correlated - the principle of consensus.

When using corporate pluralism as categorising democratic systems, three levels of consensus were pointed out in the introduction: basic, procedural and policy consensus. The empirical part of this work nonetheless deals with the third level of consensus, i.e. policy consensus. Policy consensus can be regarded as based on deliberative processes as forms of discussions '... intended to change the preferences of the bases on which people decide how to act'.[1] The ideal objective of deliberation is consequently to aim at rationally motivated consensus where reasons persuasive to all are sought. If such a consensus cannot be found, decisions have to be made by voting.[2] From this, it also follows that if all reasons and

[1] Przeworski 1998, 140.

[2] Cohen 1989, 23.

arguments have been presented and a decision has been made, but there are still individuals who do not agree to the final decision, then they are coerced to act against their reasons.[1] Consensus is therefore not the same as consent. Consensus refers to a generally accepted opinion among a group of people, while consent refers to the opinions of individuals. Although there may be consensus on a policy issue, it does not necessarily have to have the consent of all involved individuals. As Elder et al. also noted, no politician voluntarily seeks consensus – it has to be forced upon him.[2] The third level of consensus is therefore where dissent, dissensus and opposition emerges.

The aim of this book is as noted in the introduction, to analyse how dissent, dissensus and opposition has been dealt with in the context of corporate pluralist arrangements. Such an analysis is important not least from a normative perspective. The normative aspect of corporate pluralist arrangements have frequently been stressed by politicians, when a recurring subject in parliamentary debates on working life issues has been the decisive influence of the main economic interest groups in the preparatory legislative work. This debate has nonetheless been a neglected phenomenon by political scientists. According to Ricci, the tragedy of political science has been a shift from normatively charged questions to the empirically 'manageable' where political scientists have turned away from questions that politicians and ordinary citizens regard as important. The normatively charged concepts of 'good', 'evil', 'justice', 'rights', 'patriotic' etc. have been replaced by neutral concepts of 'attitude', 'conflict', 'game', 'interaction' etc. Scientists have been speaking among themselves in terms of jargons, not to the public.[3] The aim of this part of the chapter is to evaluate how corporate pluralist arrangements can be normatively justified as a means in building consensus, and relate this justification to the practice of consensus building. This forms the empirical part of this thesis. The argument therefore entails a comparison between what should be done, to what is actually done in practice.

Normative discussions naturally imply that no definite answers are possible. It is a question of arguments versus counterarguments. In evaluating the normative basis for corporate pluralism, one therefore has to analyse what arguments can be expressed in favour of corporate pluralist arrangements as a desirable (good) way of reaching consensus, and what

---

[1] Przeworski 1998, 142.

[2] Elder et al. 1982, 159.

[3] Ricci 1984, 296-299.

the counterarguments are that regard them as an undesirable (bad) way of consensus. The problem can be related to whether the process before a consensus is eventually reached is normatively more important than the substance of the outcomes.[1] The first question to be asked is therefore whether the ends are more important than the means.

Means versus Ends

As noted earlier, corporate pluralist arrangements were in analyses by political economists often seen as means in creating economic growth and stability. They were not convinced, however, that the arrangements had any effect on economic performance. If they would have been convinced of this effect, corporate pluralism could consequently have been normatively justified as an acceptable means. Corporate pluralist arrangements in Sweden were also regarded as a means leading to social integration of the minority interests. Even if the minority interests had not been accepted in the parliamentary channel, where majority rules, they still had a second opportunity through the influence of organised interests in the corporate pluralist channel. The accommodation of minorities through this channel had therefore reduced the prospects for conflicts and enabled a development of stable democracy. They have been a good means to a desirable end. From the opposite perspective, however, the corporate pluralist arrangements have been seen as resulting in a democratic deficit, where the parliament has been reduced to a rubber-stamp on economic and labour market issues. Governments have made 'deals' with the main economic interest groups, in order to work for long-term economic policies.

The minor importance of the parliament in corporate pluralist arrangements is the main reason why the arrangements have been regarded by many in a negative light. The arrangements have functioned alongside the parliamentary work, not justified according to any legislation, and closed to public scrutiny. The normative question is, however, whether parliamentary decisions are needed if the same regulations can be made differently, but with the same results for the people and society? The problem is consequently how to know that the outcome is good for the people, what interests are to be favoured, and which institutions can best protect these interests?[2] The parliament has an advantage because it allows for public discussions and debates. Processes of consensus building in

---

[1] Dahl 1989, 180.

[2] Dahl 1989, 180.

corporate pluralist contexts depend on how the elites are able to accommodate conflicts and are consequently closed to public scrutiny. If the (parliamentary) democratic deficit has been overtaken by interest organisational knowledge in the process, corporate pluralism may be seen as normatively acceptable. In that case, the knowledge of the main economic interest groups complements their representative function. If the democratic deficit, on the other hand, has been overtaken by the use of mere resources, then the normative justification is questionable. In that case the interests taking part in the decision making processes focus mainly on control, i.e. how to secure their own interests, without necessarily taking into account the common good. The crucial normative justification of corporate pluralism is therefore to be based on the concept of knowledge, and how it has been used/misused by the participants in the process.

Knowledge versus Power

The building of modern welfare states after world war two meant that the amount of social and economic issues that the state has to deal with greatly increased. It was therefore necessary to involve the knowledge of different interests, since important economic and social interests could easily be harmed if decisions were left only to political and administrative organs. In a corporate pluralist context, the main economic interest groups were consequently involved in different kinds of committees, commissions, and boards as well as the remiss-system as bearers of knowledge. The problem with a concept like knowledge is that it can be seen both in normative and empirical terms. In normative terms it can be regarded as knowledge about what is morally acceptable for a society. This kind of knowledge becomes highly subjective in character, since people differ in their views of what is good for a society. (What is morally acceptable in modern Western capitalist democracies may not be morally acceptable in many Islamic countries.) Knowledge in empirical terms can on the other hand be regarded as empirically based understanding about how to achieve desired ends. The justification of the inclusion of the main economic interest groups is therefore to be based mainly on their possession of empirical knowledge.

When it comes to corporate pluralist arrangements another problem that arises and needs to be addressed is the relationship between knowledge and power. Is it possible to combine reasoned arguments with power in the name of consensus building? Powerful participants taking part in the corporate pluralist arrangements do not necessarily have to rely on consensus to the same extent as resourceless ones, because reason is the only source of power the powerless have.[1] The question consequently becomes what rationalities the participants in the decision making process have used in order to build consensus. For example, have they argued according to their knowledge of the issue, have they used their resources (threats of strikes, lockouts and other activities) to influence the outcome, have they resorted to expert-evaluations of the issue or have they simply justified their arguments by the interests of their members? By evaluating these kinds of questions, it should be possible to say something about the process of reaching consensus and how the participants have used their power and knowledge in the process. If, for example, they have merely used their resources and power in the process in order to work for their own interests, then the normative justification of corporate pluralism as a good way of policy making is questionable. Basically, it is therefore a problem of whether knowledge as an essential feature of a good polity is possible, or whether knowledge only becomes another tool in the execution of power. If, as Flyvbjerg (1988) argues, knowledge becomes distorted by power, consensus also becomes difficult to achieve as the more powerful do not have to rely only on their knowledge, but can also use their resources in order to achieve their preferences.[2] In that case, dissent, dissensus and opposition has been overruled by the use of power, rather than by rational arguments that everyone can accept.

Conclusions

If focusing on corporate pluralist arrangements in a context of consensual democracy, the arrangements imply a procedural consensus when the elites of the main economic interest groups, together with the government, have been able to conclude settlements that have been approved by all parties. Although the end products of corporate pluralist arrangements have been characterised by inclusion and compromise, the question is whether this also means that the negotiations themselves between the elites have been characterised by a search for consensus. How has dissensus and opposition been dealt with in the decision making process? Another problem that needs to be addressed is whether there is consensus at all. Despite the fact that the end products may seem consensual in character, there may still be

---

[1] Flyvbjerg 1998, 229-233.

[2] Flyvbjerg 1998, 229-230.

participants in the processes that due to lack of resources, or other circumstances, have been coerced to comply with the decision. In such a case it would be premature to state that the decision is based on consensus.

Returning to the research question, the analysis of the working hours case should, therefore, provide information about how dissent, dissensus and opposition was dealt with in the decision making process. The analysis should also provide information about whether the normative justifications of corporate pluralist arrangements, as a means of including knowledge into the process, are sustainable. This can only be done by an in-depth analysis of decision making processes, in this case the development of the working hours legislation. Before that the next chapter will make an inductive approach to the relationship between the main economic interest groups and governments, and evaluate what the development of working hours regulations can tell about Finnish interest intermediation.

3 Working Hours and Interest Intermediation in Finland – a Politics of Accommodation?

As shown in the previous chapter, it is debatable whether the concept of corporatism provided for any theoretical advancement to the established pluralist forms of interest intermediation, and whether the concept provided for any increased understanding on how the regularised relationship between governments and the main economic interest groups worked in practice. Instead of trying to explain the development of interest intermediation in Finland by reference to the concept of corporatism, a more fruitful approach is to start with the empirical, in this case the working hours regulations. The first aim of this chapter is therefore to evaluate what the development of working hours regulations can tell about the broad picture of interest intermediation on the labour market in Finland. The second aim is an analysis of whether there is a model of Finnish interest intermediation that can be regarded as having become institutionalised. A question of whether a model has become institutionalised or not is important, since, according to a neo-institutional theoretical framework, institutions are vital in explaining political behaviour.

The Development of Working Hours Regulations in Finland

The development of working hours regulations in Finland can crudely be divided into two main stages. The first is the development from early industrialisation in the nineteenth century, up to 1944, when basic regulations were developed. This stage can be seen as representing a form of non-regularised pressure group politics, when the main economic interest groups played no role in the actual decision making on working hours legislation. The second stage is the development after 1944, when these groups started to conclude their own general agreements.

Before the Corporate Pluralist Era

During the industrialisation era in the nineteenth and early twentieth century, the most important reasons behind the need for reduced working hours were physical. In order to increase the operating hours of machines, and so production, working hours were prolonged. Time discipline and time keeping had become the key characteristics of a labour market based on predictability, regularity and synchronisation of production and maximisation of output.[1] Early studies of work places also showed that long workdays had a detrimental effect on workers' health. In addition, the use of children at industrial work was widespread and they normally worked the same hours as adults. As a result, many of them had become unable to work because of ill health before the age of 18. In Finland, the percentage of workers under 15 years of age in the whole industrial workforce increased from 12.4 per cent in 1845, to 26.4 per cent in 1865. The problem was dealt with by a Committee for Promoting the Industry, which was set up in 1857. The conclusion of the committee did not focus on protecting children at industrial work, but proposed a restriction by child labour merely in order to enable employers to increase production. The committee's proposal did not lead to any regulations. In a subsequent debate in the Diet in 1868 on a trade and industry bill, arguments were expressed both on whether employers gained any advantages by using child labour, as well as whether industrial work endangered children's health. The bill was enacted, and the first legislative statements on working hours, therefore, concerned the use of child labour in the industrial sector. The law set the minimum age of workers at 12, whilst night work was prohibited for workers under 18. As a result, the percentage of workers under 15 years of age had fallen to 19.6 per cent in 1882. In a revision of the law in 1909, the minimum age was set at 14 years. By this time, the revision did not cause much discussion.[2] The lack of interest intermediation in the mid-nineteenth century was therefore reflected in these debates, which were not primarily concerned with labour protection, but rather with the productivity and efficiency of the industry.

[1] Blyton 1985, 1.

[2] Tiitinen et al. 1996, 2-4.

Demands for general eight-hour working days for adults had also been made by the International Workingmen's Association in the 1860s, and similar demands were made in Finland at the end of the nineteenth century.[1] The Social Democratic Party was formed in 1899 and demanded at its inaugural meeting an introduction of a regulation on eight-hour working days. It was not until 1908, however, that the first comprehensive legislative act on working hours for adults in Finland was enacted – the Bakery Act. Working hours in the bakeries had been exceptionally long, and in this act, it was stated that the upper limit of working hours in bakeries was to be 48 hours weekly with a total limit for daily work of ten hours. The maximum amount of overtime was also set at 100 hours a year. The act was something of an exception, since legislative statements on working hours were still rare at this time. Agreements on working hours had previously been made by employers' independent decisions, as a result of agreements between employers and workers, or as a result of strikes.[2] Trade union policy at this time was also directed towards work for agreements on working hours between individual workers and employers. In this way, workers who were members of trade unions could benefit from reduced working hours. Membership in trade unions was at this stage still low, when under 5 per cent of the workforce was organised.

Other initiatives on eight-hour working days were introduced in 1908. MPs Sivenius et al. tabled a parliamentary bill for an eight-hour working day for state employees, MP Paasivuori tabled a bill on eight-hour working days in municipalities, and MP Ahlroos tabled a bill on eight-hour working days in the state administration.[3] An introduction of the eight-hour regulation was seen as the most important instrument in improving conditions for workers at that time. According to the MPs behind the bills, it was important that laws were introduced in order to give the same rights for unorganised workers through legislation, as the organised workers had received as a result of their membership in trade unions. There were at this stage also signs of the growing importance of the trade union movement as a political force. For example, in the bill on eight-hour working days in the state administration, it was suggested that the government should set up a committee to investigate working conditions in the state sector, with half of the seats allocated to trade union representatives.[4] The trade union

---

[1] Blyton 1989, 109.

[2] Tiitinen et al. 1996, 6.

[3] Parliamentary bills 123/1908, 142/1908, 63/1908, 81/1908.

[4] Parliamentary bill 81/1908.

movement consequently gained in importance in the early twentieth century, already indicating the first signs of interest intermediation between them and the state.

It was not until 1917 that the first general act on working hours was enacted in Finland. There had been an intense debate among workers on reduced working hours. As a result, eight-hour working days had been implemented in several industrial branches, as well as in trade and craft businesses. In addition, a legislative bill on working hours was introduced by MP Walpas-Hänninen. In the subsequent parliamentary debate, the parliamentary standing Committee for Labour Affairs responded that it was well known that the workers' health and wellbeing had suffered, because of overlong working days. The committee referred to the United States and England where regulations on working hours had already been set at eight or ten hours a day in the nineteenth century.[1] The committee suggested that regulations on eight-hour working days and 48 hour working weeks should not only be left to workers who managed to reach an agreement with their employers, but should be generally applied to the labour market. The only areas left outside the statements were to be home work, agriculture, work at sea, police and firefighter work.[2] Other important features of the new act were that the maximum amount of overtime was set at ten hours weekly, and 100 hours per year, including a limitation of work on Sundays. The parliamentary Grand Committee supported the proposal by the Committee for Labour Affairs, suggesting that the parliament approve the legislative bill, which it did on September 28, 1917.

Subsequent legislation followed in Finland, when an act on working conditions in shops and offices was enacted in 1919. Despite the title of the act, it was basically a regulation on working hours. The act was partially revised in 1921, and 1922, and totally revised in 1934. An act on working hours for seamen was enacted in 1924, and the act on working hours in bakeries was partly revised in 1928, and totally revised in 1940. It became significant for the 1930s, that a reduction of working hours was regarded an important instrument in trying to reduce the effects of an economic crisis in industrialised countries. This consequently resulted in a shift from a focus

---

[1] In Great Britain, the so-called Ten Hours Movement had started to lobby for ten hour working days for women and children in the textile industry. An Act was eventually passed in 1847 and limited the work of women and children to ten hours daily. The employers nonetheless managed to make an amendment to the act that extended women's working hours. (Blyton 1985, 108.)

[2] Report by the Committee for Labour Affairs, No. 7, 1917, 1-8.

on workers' health, to an emphasis on economic and employment factors. The goal was a reduction of working hours to between 40 and 44 hours a week. On the eve of Second World War, the normal amount worked weekly in Finland had been reduced to between 40 and 46 hours, compared to 1909 when the large majority of industrial workers still worked between 50 and 60 hours a week.[1] The working hours act from 1917 was revised in 1946.[2]

The trade unions and employers' groups played no decisive role in the actual decision making on early legislation on working hours, despite the fact that the first working hours act from 1917 had been intensely debated in the trade union movement. None of the organised interests had gained exclusive or regularised access to the decision making process and the bills were submitted by individual socialist MPs. This non-regulated nature of interest intermediaiton is not a surprising finding, since the trade union movement was still weak and the left-wing movement was divided at this time. After the civil war in 1918, Social Democrats did not start to take regular part in governments until 1937 and communist activities were suppressed until 1944.[3]

It was not until after 1944, when collective bargaining negotiations between the central confederations of trade unions and employer associations were established, that the main economic interest groups started to play a more significant role in regulating the labour market. The National Employers' Federation (STK, later TT) accepted the Central Organisation of Trade Unions (SAK) as an equal negotiating partner, and these organisations started to make their own regulations, alongside

---

[1] Tiitinen et al.1996, 6.

[2] Tiitinen et al. 1996, 8.

[3] The Finnish government had declared Finland independent from Russia in 1917. At a parliamentary election in 1916, the Social Democratic Party had won an absolute majority in parliament with 103 of a total of 200 seats. At a subsequent parliamentary election in 1917, SDP lost its majority. The party became concerned with how to control the revolutionary mood of the masses, caused by both the revolution in Russia, as well as food shortages. After the declaration of independence, despite Social Democratic opposition, the government officially declared the civil guard as the troops of the government. The Social Democrats and Communists formed the red guard, and armed confrontation was inevitable. Civil war broke out on January 27, 1918 with severe bloodshed following. The civil guard, with help from Germany, defeated the red guard. As a result, the SDP was severely damaged and communist parties became prohibited until 1944. Governments in Finland between 1918 and 1937 were therefore based on non-socialist coalitions.

legislation, for the labour market. These regulations were implemented as general agreements, the first made in 1944. Such agreements included aspects like labour protection, rationalisation, training and co-operation in companies.[1]

The Corporate Pluralist Era From 1944 to Present

After the Second World War, reduced working hours were not seen as a particularly important problem for Finland. Repaying a war debt to the Soviet Union, payable largely in form of heavy goods, meant that there was no place for any reduced working hours. It was not until the 1950s that the issue returned to the agenda. In most Western European countries, flexible working hours arrangements had been improved by giving each individual industrial section opportunities for making their own agreements on working hours. Working hours regulations were therefore made by agreement between the parties on the labour market. These agreements were either general agreements, sectoral level agreements between trade unions and employers associations, or agreements at the firm level.[2] The Finnish government appointed a working hours committee in 1954, with the task of evaluating opportunities for reduced working hours in areas where the working hours act was applied. The committee finished its work in 1957. It came to the conclusion that the amount of working hours was fairly low in Finland compared to other industrialised countries, and that it had not been proved that shortened working hours had any decisive effect on the reduction of unemployment. The committee based its conclusion on reports by ILO and a Swedish Commission of Public Investigations *(Statens Offentliga Utredningar)* on reduced working hours. The committee consequently stated that there was no need for new legislative statements on shortened working hours in Finland at that point.[3] It concluded that the best way of solving the problem of working hour reductions was to let the parties on the labour market make their own agreements.[4] Consequently, in a general agreement between the national confederations of trade unions and employers' associations, the general weekly amount of working hours was reduced to 45 in 1958.

---

[1] Helander 1983, 99.

[2] International Labour Review 1957, 477.

[3] Committee report 1957: 50, 103-105.

[4] Committee report 1957: 50, 102-103.

Another reason behind giving the parties on the labour market this authority to make agreements was to include the organised interests in public policy making.[1] A working group appointed by the prime minister in 1962 had as its task to define the role of the government in relation to both ministerial agencies and political parties, as well as to the interest groups in society. This new role was defined as social policy planning *(yhteiskuntapoliittinen suunnittelu)*. One result of the policy was that the number of committees preparing and planning welfare policy heavily increased. In 1960, there were in all 328 permanent and temporary committees. In 1965 the number had increased to 497.[2] In addition, a specific objective in the governmental programme from 1966, was to work for a 'technocratic form for preparation of matters', which meant a development of interministerial procedures and a development of the relationship between the state and organised interests.[3] This co-operation resulted in the main economic interest groups gaining an increasing access to a variety of boards and commissions where labour market issues and legislation were discussed. A revision of the working hours act in 1965 became one example of how the main economic interest groups implemented the authority they had received over revisions of labour market legislation. This also serves as a first example of consensus at the third level, i.e. policy consensus.

The need for a revision of the working hours act in the mid 1960s originated from a general agreement between the central confederations of trade unions and employers' associations. An international labour conference in 1962 had recommended that the weekly amount of working hours be reduced to 40. In negotiating for collective agreements for 1964-65, the central confederations of trade unions consequently demanded a reduction of working hours. The national conciliator of labour disputes, who led the negotiations, proposed a general agreement on 40 hours working weeks.[4] An agreement was reached on June 30, 1965 between SAK and STK. In the first section of the agreement, the parties committed themselves to a gradual reduction of working hours to 40 weekly, a reduction that was to be fully implemented by 1.1.1970. Another important paragraph in the agreement was that Saturday was to become the second

[1] Government Bill 1965: 151, 5.

[2] Helander 1983, 33.

[3] Tiihonen 1990, 247-250.

[4] Government bill 151/1965, 2.

regular weekly day off, in addition to Sunday.[1] The only condition for implementing this arrangement was that some legislative revisions to the working hours act had to be made. The reason for this was that in giving the parties on the labour market greater opportunities for making their own agreements on reduced working hours, contradictory paragraphs on, for example, the regulations on daily and weekly working hours, night work and weekly rest, had to be made.[2]

The government submitted a bill to parliament in November 1965, suggesting revisions to the existing working hours act. The main suggested revisions were that the regular working hours were to be set at eight hours a day and 40 hours a week, and that the parties on the labour market were given the rights by collective agreements to implement regulations on working hours other than the act stated. The first time these rights were introduced into legislation was in an act concerning workers' annual holidays from 1960. Subsequently, in 1966, a similar paragraph was included in the proposed revision of the working hours act, stating

> ...The confederations of trade-unions and employers associations whose activity covers the whole country may conclude collective agreements, which may include statements concerning §§ 5-6, otherwise than this act states.

The paragraph gave the national and sectoral confederations of trade unions and employers' associations rights to make their own collective agreements on the regular amount of working hours, and on a maximum of 120 hours over a three-week period in some sectors. The reason for introducing this kind of paragraph in 1966 was to include the statement on 40 hours working weeks in the general agreement in legislation. Another revision of the act concerned maximum amounts of overtime, night work, payment for overtime, work on Sundays and the date the law enters into force.[3] In December 1965, negotiations were held between the government and all the central confederations of trade unions and employers' associations. In these negotiations, the parties stated that they basically agreed with the government bill, except for some minor sentences that had to be added. They were that deviations from §6 of the act (concerning the statement of a maximum of 120 working hours over three weeks) could

---

[1] General Agreement 30.6.1965.

[2] Government bill 151/1965, 1.

[3] Government bill 151/1965.

only be made if the nature of work so demanded, or if it was required in preventing inappropriate arrangements for workers.[1]

The parliamentary standing Committee on Social Affairs and Health subsequently suggested that the bill be approved by parliament. The committee proposed the same revisions of the government bill as was agreed between the government and the main economic interest groups at their meeting. One dissenting opinion was added to the committee report. The Grand Committee made no further changes to the proposal. In the parliamentary debate, arguments in favour of and against, the involvement of the interest groups were discussed. According to one argument, the organisations in question had been regarded as showing a certain kind of maturity in their negotiations.[2] Arguments were also made, suggesting that the main economic interest groups had a decisive authority over this issue, since the revision of the act was a result of the negotiations between them and the government. According to this view, the government had been forced to make the changes, and now the parliament was regarded to be in the same situation. If the bill was not enacted before the end of the year, the main economic interest groups had threatened that there would be no new collective agreements for the different sectors on the labour market.[3] The parliament enacted the bill on December 29, 1965, according to the changes proposed by the main economic interest groups. Dissensus and opposition in the parliamentary handling of the bill did therefore not have any impact. As already mentioned in the introduction, a significant feature for the rest of the 1960s, and the 1970s was that the main economic interest groups, together with the government, made broad-based incomes policy settlements that defined the economic and labour market policy in Finland. These arrangements also resulted in extensive legislative revisions of social and labour legislation.

The introduction of a corporate pluralist form of interest intermediation can therefore be seen in terms of the relationship between labour market legislation, enacted by parliament, and general agreements, concluded between the main economic interest groups.

As shown in table 3.1, the main shift in policy consequently occurred after 1944, when the main economic interest groups started to make their own general agreements. After 1944, general agreements became the most important source of regulations on working hours and legislation merely

[1] Protocol from negotiations between the main economic interest groups, 15.12.1965.

[2] Parliamentary Protocol 21.12.1965, 2055.

[3] Parliamentary protocol 28.12.1965, 2233.

followed behind, adapting to what had been concluded between the main economic interest groups. The main source of regulation had consequently shifted from legislation to agreements made between the parties on the labour market.

Table 3.1 The development of general working hours regulations in Finland

1868	Law on working hours for children
1908	First law on working hours for adults (Bakery Act)
1917	First general eight-hour working hours law
1944	First general agreement between SAK and STK
1958	General agreement on 45 hours working weeks
1965	General agreement on 40 hours working weeks
1966	Revised working hours act on 40 hours working weeks

After the reduction to 40 working hours per week in 1970, the issue did not come up again until the mid-1980s when Finnish trade unions demanded reduced working hours. The employers initially opposed this, and instead demanded an introduction of more flexible working hours. In the prosperous economic climate in Finland in the mid- to late 1980s, the employers nonetheless eventually agreed to reduced working hours. This reduction was contained in the 1986 incomes policy settlements, and it covered workers with 40-hour working weeks. In the settlement, it was stated that the yearly amount of working hours was to be reduced by 16 hours in 1987, 1988 and 1989 and by 20 hours in 1990 respectively.[1] (These reductions have been called 'Pekkas-days' *(Pekkas-päivät)*, named after Mauri Pekkanen, who led the negotiations.) The working hours act was also revised once during the 1980s. In this revision, a new paragraph was introduced on the so-called flexitime, enabling more individual working hour arrangements. This paragraph gave the employers and workers opportunities for making agreements on how to arrange the start and finish of their day, according to personal needs. This flexitime could be a maximum of two hours per day. The total amount of working hours was not to be reduced, however. The revision would not have been possible without the good economic situation in Finland in the late 1980s.[2]

[1] Incomes policy settlement 15.3.1986, 2.

[2] Interview with a representative of national trade union (STTK) 11.11.1997.

In the 1980s, employers also demanded that the whole working hours act was to be revised in order to meet new demands on the labour market for more flexibility. As noted in the introduction, the government programme from 1987 stated that the government, led by the Conservatives, was going to evaluate opportunities for revising the working hours legislation together with the parties on the labour market. All parties agreed to the setting up of a committee, which would conduct the preparatory work for a revision. The initiative was also included in the broad-based incomes policy settlement for 1990-91, negotiated in autumn 1989. The government consequently appointed the working hours committee in 1990.

A Finnish Form of Labour Market Interest Intermediation?

It is obvious that the pattern of interest intermediation between governments and the main economic interest groups changed after 1944. The early non-regularised forms of interest intermediation changed into something resembling corporatism, corporate pluralism or liberal corporatism. The problem with corporatism as theoretical concept was, however, that it did not provide for much advancement to the pluralist forms of interest intermediation. Leaving the concepts of corporatism and pluralism aside, the aim of the second part of this chapter is a focus on whether there is a model of interest intermediation between governments and the main economic interest groups. As noted in the introduction, the large coalition governments, the absence of ideological polarisation between parties, the less intense conflicts between consumer and producer interests, and the broad-based incomes policy settlements, can all be regarded as pointing towards an establishment of a politics of elite accommodation in Finland.

A Politics of Elite Accommodation

A politics of accommodation basically means that different opinions are taken into account and accommodated with the opinions of the majority. Such a politics is closely related to the consociational democracies, which is a non-economic model of government, based on an idea of a search for pragmatic solutions in plural societies characterised by irreconcilable opposing segments and views.[1] The political elite is able to counteract the destabilising effect of cultural fragmentation and consequently enable a development of stable democracy. The elites have to co-operate with each other and make compromises without losing the allegiance of their rank and file supporters.[2] Consociationalism is therefore aiming at an accommodation of different views at the elite level. Corporate pluralist arrangements and consociationalism denotes similar features. In consociational systems the elites of sub-cultural interests are able to co-operate and bridge conflicts, while in corporatist systems the functional interests on the labour market, together with governments, are able to co-operate in order to work for a stable economic and labour market development.[3]

It is obvious that Finland lacks the most important characteristic of consociational democracy – the necessary cleavage structure of society, although there have been some tendencies for such cleavages over the years, like for example the civil war, mentioned earlier, and subsequent exclusion of communist activities between 1918 and 1944. Another example of a cleavage has been the language issue (Finland was a part of the Swedish empire until 1809 and has remained a bilingual country with Finnish and Swedish mentioned in the constitution). A third example of a cleavage is the rural-urban issue. This issue mainly concerned producer vs. consumer interests in terms of pricing policy of agricultural products, state subsidies and private ownership of land.

Although Finland cannot be regarded as a consociational democracy, the politics of elite accommodation can be operationalised by using some of Lijphart's categories from 1968. When it comes to the Finnish labour market, the principle of proportionality, which deals with an even allocation of scarce financial resources between different segments in society, and rules of the game, which relates to decision making procedures, are relevant.[4] (The minority veto before the constitutional amendment in 1992, mentioned in the introduction, can also be related to the rules of the game.) On the principle of proportionality, the whole population has been included in some way or another in the broad-based settlements through an equal allocation of benefits. For example, the last settlement for 1998-2000 covered over 98 per cent of the whole labour

---

[1] Lijphart 1968.

[2] Lijphart 1969, 211-212, 221.

[3] Scholten 1987, 4.

[4] Lijphart 1977, 38.

market. In addition, the farmers have had their own negotiations and detailed agreements (under the umbrella of broad-based income policy settlements) with the Ministry of Agriculture. Up to the 1990s the proportionality on income was related to an allocation of scarce values. In the 1995, and to some extent the 1997 settlement, it was more a question of low or no wage increases in exchange for low price increases. Economic policy during the 1990s has largely been based on wage-freeze and extensive cuts in public spending. During the discussions on whether there should be a broad-based settlement after the last one expired 31.12.1999, demands for individual collective agreements for each sector of the labour market were often expressed. As noted in the introduction, despite the fact that a majority of the trade unions supported a continued broad-based incomes policy settlement for 2000-01, some influential unions did not agree to any settlement, and it consequently failed. The main reason why they did not agree to any broad-based settlement was that they demanded a higher wage increase than such a settlement would have allowed for.

The introduction of broad-based income policy settlements does not only correlate with the proportionality-feature but also with different rules of the game. Such rules were not as important as the other features of consociational democracy, but were more a mix of general procedures. During the incomes policy era the negotiations around the settlements were compatible with the most important rule for a spirit of accommodation: 'the business of politics'. Politics was to be regarded as serious work where the political elite should be oriented towards results and where disputes should not stand in the way of getting the job done. Between 1968 and 1974 the Finnish governments received rights, by the so-called Acts of Authority *(valtuuslaki)*, to produce the desired objectives of the incomes policy settlements.[1] These acts were approved for one to two years at a time. The exact content of them was settled in negotiations between governments and the main economic interest groups. The acts also meant a significant delegation of legislative power to the government. It was stated that if certain governmental decisions made according to the act demanded the parliament's approval, the government's decision had to be immediately submitted to the parliamentary speaker. The parliament thereafter had to deal with the matter as soon as possible and either approve or reject the proposal. This was a typical way of handling labour market matters during

---

[1] This Act is a reminiscent of war time legislation where special Acts of Authority were approved in order to give the government extended power in states of emergency.

the time these acts were in force.[1] The parliament thus formally made the final decisions but the factual power to make these decisions was in the hands of the government and main economic interest groups.[2]

Does it then matter whether a Finnish form of interest intermediation is characterised by an elite accommodation? According to the neo-institutional theoretical framework, it does. If corporatism has remained a widely used concept since the early to mid-1970s, the concept of institutions has since the mid-1980s, according to neo-institutionalism, become an important feature of politics. The basic idea behind neo-institutionalism is that institutions are not solely dependent on human action, but they also determine and shape individual behaviour themselves.[3] The Cambridge dictionary of English (1995) provides for an accurate definition of institutions as 'a custom, system or organisation that has existed for a long time and is accepted as an important part of particular society'. From a narrow perspective, institutions can therefore be defined as large and important organisations. From a wide perspective, they can be defined as social customs that have reached a certain stage. In the latter sense, institutions are not dependent on recurrent collective mobilisations in order to exist.[4]

There are several reasons why the elite accommodation in Finland can be regarded as having become institutionalised. The paragraph that was introduced into the working hours law, quoted earlier, has meant that collective agreements between the parties on the labour market has become institutionalised, since it is a paragraph in a Finnish law. It is not merely a temporary rule, like the Acts of Authority between 1968 and 1975, but included in the permanent working hours law. If, hypothetically, the paragraph is to be withdrawn or revised, it requires the consent of the central confederations of trade unions, since they have an automatic access to preparatory work on revisions to labour market legislation. Such consent would be highly unlikely at the moment.

Interest intermediation in Finland can also be related to neo-institutionalism in the sense that it would be impossible to leave the main economic interest groups out from arenas where labour market issues are discussed. This feature has thus become something of an informal rule and practice, which determines government behaviour. It resembles what has

---

[1] Myllymäki 1979, 57-58.

[2] Myllymäki 1979, 213-214.

[3] March and Olsen 1984; 1989.

[4] Jepperson 1991, 144.

been called normative institutionalism, which regarded institutions as collections of norms, rules and routines that defined the appropriate action in terms of relations between roles and situations.[1] March and Olsen regarded it as acting according to a logic of appropriateness. In a logic of appropriateness, behaviour involves fulfilling the obligations of a role in a situation and that action can be more defined by duties and obligations than a behaviour according to consequences. What is appropriate for one person in a situation is defined by political and social institutions. A seeking of specific rules involves an analysis of the characteristics of a specific situation and the choices involve a comparison of a situation with a behaviour that fits into the situation.[2] For example, during the Cuba crisis, President Kennedy had to choose between naval blockade, air attack or land invasion. The reason for this was not that these were the only options, but because these were the routines worked out by Pentagon.[3] Similarily, it would since 1944 not be an option to leave the main economic interest groups out of processes where labour market issues have been discussed in Finland. Their participation has become a routine in itself.

The inclusion of the main economic interest groups as advisers in various committees after 1944, as well as the conclusion of broad based incomes policy settlements since 1968, still exist as an important phenomenon of Finnish politics. This can also be related to the concept of historical institutionalism, which emphasises the persistence of organisations after they have been formed, and the importance and persistence of institutional structures in shaping policies over time.[4] The way in which the revision of the working hours act was conducted in 1965 would, furthermore, point to a rational institutionalism. Rational institutionalism is a kind of an antithesis to the normative institutionalism in that it assumes the importance of rational human behaviour. This form of neo-institutionalism stresses that individuals realise the constraints and opportunities institutions create, and they can use them in attempts to maximise their outcomes.[5] During the negotiations between the main economic interest groups and the government in 1965 on a revision of the working hours act, the interest groups took advantage of the negotiations with the government, and pushed through their own preferences, which

---

[1] March and Olsen 1989, 21.

[2] March and Olsen 1989, 24-25.

[3] Allison 1971. (For more examples, see March and Olsen 1989, 95-116.)

[4] Peters 1999, 67.

[5] Peters 1999, 45.

were later approved without changes by the parliament. Regardless of which variant of these institutionalist approaches is applied, it seems fairly safe to state that the elite accommodation in Finland has become institutionalised.

The argument that the elites have been accommodated is, however, only based on the political structures. If analysing individual policy issues, the picture may be different. Despite the accommodation at the elite level, it does not necessarily mean that individual policy issues have to be characterised by accommodation.

A Politics of Non-Accommodation

The argument that a politics of elite accommodation has to be viewed in relation to individual policy issues is underlined by three examples. The first one is the thesis that a close and regularised relationship between the main economic interest groups and governments lead to a decline in strike activity, because the accommodating politics at the elite level reach solutions that involve a large part of the population.[1] A second example is the policy implemented since 1996 by the Centre Party, which has been the largest party in opposition since 1995. The third example is the question of whether Finland should join the European Monetary Union.

Strike activity Despite the fact that governments and the main economic interest groups have continuously agreed on broad-based incomes policy settlements in Finland, they do not have unconditional support from the individual trade unions. In addition, the basic divisions in society between labour and capital are still highly relevant. There is still a strong belief in collective action and solidarity among workers, plus a strong belief in flexible, non-standard arrangements among employers. These divisions have been underlined by both SAK's and the semi-independent Finnish Centre for Business and Policy Studies (EVA) surveys and should therefore be fairly accurate.[2] A great majority (79 per cent) of the public who took part in one survey regarded collective efforts as the most important mean for success, while a minority (35 per cent) regarded the market economy as having developed in a positive direction. An almost total majority (94 per cent) of the workforce was of the opinion that the minimum regulations on

[1] Lewin 1994.

[2] EVA is the main institution producing material for business, originally founded by the large business organisations in 1974.

working conditions were to be made collectively, while the managers of companies were highly critical towards a solidaristic wage policy.[1] The contemporary discourse in western democracies, largely focusing on competitiveness and business productivity, does therefore not have much support among ordinary Finnish workers.[2]

This is also reflected in strike activity in Finland, indicating that the regularised relationships between governments and the main economic interest groups have not created a consensus at the workplace level.

Table 3.2 Number of industrial conflicts, workers affected and working days lost by industrial disputes 1968-97

Year	Industrial disputes	Workers Affected	Working days lost
1968-72	2153	964,600	3,860,800
1973-77	9282	2,520,500	6,916,100
1978-82	8080	1,467,160	2,848,100
1983-87	6525	1,857,690	5,339,390
1988-92	1669	917,590	1,853,610
1993-97	594	292,284	1,536,221

Source: Statistical Yearbook of Finland 1998

It would be difficult to explain the decline in strike activity by the regularised relationship between the main economic interest groups and governments, since strike activity heavily increased in the early 1970s, despite the conclusion of broad-based settlements. (Data from before 1971 are not comparable because of the use of a different statistical method.) The years 1971, 1973, 1977, and 1986 were the most strike active in terms of

---

[1] EVA Report 1997; SAK Työelämätieto 2/98, 15; SAK Tutkimustieto hösten 1998, 4.

[2] Similar tendencies can also be found in the other Scandinavian countries. Studies of data from the 1970s and 1980s from Norway, Sweden and Denmark provide great support for the hypothesis that left-right materialism constituted the major value orientation among the public. Similar findings were also found in the UK, although they did not support the left-right materialism dichotomy as clearly as the Scandinavian countries. According to left-wing materialist values, governments should play an active role in securing notions of economic security, solidarity and equality in incomes between social classes. Right-wing materialism, on the other hand, stresses the supremacy of the market and economic competition between independent enterprises. (Knutsen 1995, 160-167.)

working days lost. Another notable finding is that strike activity has been fairly low during the 1990s, despite the fact that the Finnish economy has experienced its worst recession since the Second World War. This is an interesting finding in comparison to Sweden.

Against the backdrop of a deep economic recession, the labour market in Sweden in the 1930s had become characterised by numerous strikes and lockouts, which were seen as a serious threat against a favourable economic development. Despite attempts from the government to promote peace on the labour market, it was not until the National Employers' Association (SAF) and the Central Confederation of Trade Unions (LO) signed the so-called *Saltsjöbaden-accord* in 1938 that the labour market parties started to solve conflicts peacefully, and without interference from the government. Although it had not been the intentions of SAF and LO, from now on the co-operation between governments and the main economic interest groups provided solid ground for a successful Swedish welfare state. Strikes were avoided, unemployment was insignificant, the price level remained steady, economic growth was continuous and incomes were levelled. Lewin's hypothesis for Sweden was that 'the more corporatist the decision-making process, the more successful welfare policy will be, in the sense that outcome corresponds with intent'.[1] After this period of co-operation between employers and workers, conflicts started to arise again on the Swedish labour market in the 1970s. In addition, corporate pluralist arrangements with close co-operation between governments and the main economic interest groups in Sweden, have been on a decline since the 1970s. Corporate pluralist arrangements in Sweden were no longer seen as able to succeed in fulfilling its most important moral and political task: 'to pacify intense minorities and promote social integration'.[2] Lewin's thesis on corporate pluralist arrangements as promoting peace on the labour market does consequently not have much support in a Finnish context. The explanatory value of corporate pluralism in Finland also becomes less significant.

The work reform The main problem in the development of the working hours legislation was how to combine flexible working hours demanded by employers, with collective agreements advocated by the workers' representatives. This has not only been a feature of working hours regulations, but is also a common theme in a 'work reform' *(työreformi)*

---

[1] Lewin 1994, 66.

[2] Lewin 1994, 73-75.

presented by the Centre Party. The background to the reform, first published in 1996, was that, according to the Party, new measures were needed in order to create more employment. Merely low wage increases and a fight against inflation was not enough, but more structural changes were required. The Party wanted to increase the opportunities for unemployed to become part of the labour market, instead of being long term unemployed, having to take early retirement or resorting merely to various educational courses.[1] The work reform became the Centre Party's main political programme before the 1999 parliamentary election.

The Party presented six general points on how to achieve a higher level of employment. According to the Party, the sectoral collective agreements had become outdated and new measures were therefore required in order to re-structure the Finnish labour market system. In order to achieve this, the necessary means would be to make changes in unemployment security by introducing a renewed mandatory unemployment insurance scheme. This would create a more flexible system than the present one, which favours unemployed with more work experience. A second measure would be to enable people to be better able to support themselves, instead of having to resort to social allowance. This would according to the Party be possible by, for example, redefining work and thereby including homework. A third measure would be to renew the income tax system by channelling tax incomes to measures that create employment. A fourth measure would be to lower employers' employment taxes for low-wage work, and a fifth to reduce unnecessary bureaucracy when new companies are created. It was the sixth proposal, which dealt with opportunities for individual workers and employers to make firm level agreements, which created most of the controversy.

The motivation behind the proposal for increased opportunities for firm level agreements in the reform was that all employers and workers should have the same possibility to make firm level agreements, not only those who were members of trade unions and employers' associations. They therefore questioned the general implementation of the principle of universal commitment on the Finnish labour market. The reform suggested that if the employers and workers in individual firms were unable to reach an agreement, the collective agreements or legislation would provide the norms that were to be applied. The reform did not state which aspects could not be included into the firm level agreements, but it said that, for example, worker's protection and health issues were issues that could not be agreed

[1] Keskustan työreformi 30.11.1998, 1-2.

upon between individual workers and employers. Such issues had to be dealt with collectively. The sectoral collective agreements were to remain the starting point, but due to special demands in different branches, these could be complemented by firm level agreements. According to the reform, the main objective of such procedures would be to enable flexibility during times when companies faced difficulties. The introduction of flexibility in the 1990s had, in the views of the Centre Party, taken place only based on what had been stated in the sectoral collective agreements. The reform therefore sought to include the parties that were not covered by any collective agreements.[1]

The content of the work reform was therefore much in line with the current trend in the labour market, where flexible arrangements are regarded as becoming more central in the future. The Party's main antagonists could be detected at the end of the version of the work reform that was presented in 1998, in the run-up to the 1999 parliamentary election. The Party noted that the implementation of the work reform also demanded a change of the central role played by the main economic interest groups, since the important labour market interest representation would be removed from the national to the firm level.[2] According to the Party, it was no longer guaranteed that the sectoral collective agreements provided the basic labour protection in the 1990s, as had earlier been the case.

The reform was flatly rejected by the central confederations of trade unions. SAK made a polemical reply in November 1998 when it stated that the reform would

> ...break down the system where collective agreements are binding for all. The worker would have to negotiate alone with the employer about his working conditions and it would become possible to demand agreements that were less favourable than what was stated in the collective agreements. From this would follow a return to guardianship *(isäntävalta)* and a crofting society *(torppariaika)*.[3]

The Centre Party replied by noting that it was obvious that SAK dismissed the reform as such, because of its intolerance against any questioning of the sectoral collective agreements.[4] It is also worth

[1] Keskustan työreformi 30.11.1998, 13-15.

[2] Keskustan työreformi 30.11.1998, 15.

[3] SAK Julkilausuma 21.11.1998.

[4] Hufvudstadsbladet 22.11.1998.

mentioning that the strong rejection of the reform was made three months before the parliamentary election in 1999. At the end of its pamphlet, SAK also encouraged its members to vote for equality and co-operation instead of inequality and conflict.[1] SAK in practice therefore encouraged people to vote for the socialist parties and not for the Centre Party. Despite the fact that the reform dealt with other aspects than collective versus flexible agreements, this was the issue that labelled it.

The reform has not been at the forefront of the Centre Party's opposition policy since the parliamentary election in 1999, and it is currently revising the reform. The Party has waited for a solution of the revision of the employment contract act, which also dealt with the principle of universal commitment. After the revision of this act has been finalised, it will take a new standpoint as regards the work reform. The Party will also make more detailed comments to specific issues in the revised employment contract act.[2] This has therefore been another example of a non-accommodation of alternative views and opinions.

The EMU issue The broad based incomes policy settlement concluded in Finland in 1998 was connected to the question of EMU. The main justification for concluding the settlement was that it was regarded as an important means in the continuation of a favourable economic development, combined with a low inflation. It was also explicitly stated that the incomes policy settlements would be in force after the introduction of the EMU.[3] The main reason that the settlement was concluded was therefore principally to facilitate membership in the EMU. Despite the fact that the settlement enabled stable prices and moderate wage increases, it had no unconditional support among the parties on the labour market. The Social Democratic chairperson from the parliamentary Committee for Labour Affairs, who had long experience from work as a shop steward in the paper industry before becoming an MP, also noted that the support on the labour market for a second broad-based settlement in 1997 had been weak. After five years of public savings and low wage increases, several of the profitable sectors on the labour market made their explicit wishes of concluding their own individual collective agreements. This would have meant higher wage increases than the broad-based settlements allowed for. This could possibly also have led to higher inflation, and threatened the

[1] SAK Julkilausuma 21.11.1998.

[2] Interview with MP Matti Vanhanen 10.2.2000.

[3] Incomes policy settlement 1998-99, 6.

Finnish fulfilment of the criteria for membership in the EMU. The Social Democratic led government nonetheless reached an agreement with the main economic interest groups, and the individual trade unions eventually signed the settlement. In other words, consensus between the government and main economic interest groups was reached on the issue.

Table 3.3 Support for membership in EMU (percentage)

	For		Against	
	1997	1998	1997	1998
Finland	33	53	62	38
Sweden	34	39	56	50

Source: Eurobarometer 48 (autumn 1997) and 49 (spring 1998)

At the same time as the political elite managed to build consensus on the issue, the public support for EMU made a radical up-turn. Opinion polls from autumn 1997, indicated that only 33 per cent of those surveyed in Finland were in favour of membership in the EMU, while 62 per cent were against. Comparative figures for Sweden were 34 per cent for, and 56 per cent against membership. In spring 1998, 53 per cent were in favour of the EMU in Finland, and only 38 per cent against. In Sweden, 39 per cent were in favour, and 50 per cent against. The same opinion poll also indicated that only 35 per cent of the surveyed from Finland regarded EU as a whole a good thing, but 53 per cent nonetheless supported the EMU. The comparative figures for Sweden were 31 per cent, regarding EU a good thing, and 39 per cent supporting the EMU.[1] These are interesting findings. In another opinion poll, in June 1997, 46 per cent of the surveyed in Finland thought they were well informed about the Euro, whilst 53 per cent thought they were not very well informed. In February 1998, 36 per cent thought they were well informed, whilst 63 per cent thought they were not.[2] According to these opinion polls, a decrease in the opinion of how well informed they were of EMU coincided with a rapid increase in support for the EMU. This unavoidably leads to a questioning of the reliability of these surveys.

[1] Eurobarometer 48 (autumn 1997) and 49 (spring 1998).

[2] Europinion special edition (January 1999).

The public support for EMU made it easier for the government to push forward an application for membership – it merely became a question of *how* to achieve membership, not whether it was the most appropriate. This is reflected in how the decision about joining the EMU was made. The government's policy was that the decision on adopting the single currency was to be made by parliament. It regarded the best way of doing this was in the form of a so-called statement procedure *(tiedonanto)* according to §36 of the Parliament Act. This paragraph states that statement procedures can be submitted by the government to parliament on issues that relate to foreign affairs. The matter is then to be postponed to a following plenum, where it is debated. When the matter has been debated, the parliamentary speaker declares that: 'After having received the statement report, the parliament returns to the agenda'. Statement reports are therefore to be regarded as less important matters than the handling of ordinary government bills, which require three separate readings in parliament. Keeping in mind that in this case it was a question of a possible membership in EMU (and a gradual dissolution of the Finnish currency), the procedure was remarkably simple and straightforward.

This is an interesting development, as in 1995, the government stated in the programme for its term in office that '...the parliament would decide whether to participate in EMU on the basis of a separate government bill'.[1] During the referendum campaign in 1994 for membership in the European Union (EU), the question of membership in a monetary union was also downplayed, leaving the impression that it was a future project. According to the Social Democratic minister of trade and industry (1999-), if the yes-vote for membership in EU also had meant a binding decision to join the single currency, it is likely that the majority behind joining the EU in 1994 would have turned into a minority.[2] The government therefore changed its policy and in 1998 regarded a statement report as sufficient. In the first sentence of its report the government stated

> In the government's view, Finland should become a part of the Euro-area from January 1st 1999....The government asks the parliament for its opinion on a Finnish membership on the basis of this statement report.[3]

---

[1] Government programme 1995.

[2] Tuomioja 4.5.1999.

[3] Report by the government 1/98, 19.2.1998.

It was therefore not a question of whether Finland should become a member, but merely a 'message' to the parliament, that membership was the one and only possible solution for Finland. The procedure advocated by the government was implemented, and the issue was decided by parliament according to a statement procedure. The parties in opposition heavily objected to this procedure and demanded that the issue be re-opened for a new debate, and handled as a normal government bill. Although the government as such favoured membership, both the Greens and the Left Wing Alliance (former Communists) had problems in keeping all their MPs behind the government's policy line. The Greens, for example, supported a membership in EMU, but regarded a public referendum on the issue as necessary. The parties in government kept to its official line, however, and only two MPs representing the Greens, three representing the Left Wing Alliance and one representing the Social Democrats voted against the government's report, and thereby against membership. Of the other parties in government, all Conservative and Swedish People's Party MPs voted in favour of the report. All MPs representing the largest opposition Party (Centre Party) voted against the government. In all, 135 MPs voted in favour and 61 against membership, and Finland consequently applied for membership of the EMU, after a single reading in parliament. The large parliamentary backing of the government made the outcome obvious.

The procedure behind the approval of membership of the EMU in Finland significantly differs from how the issue was handled in Sweden. The main difference between Finland and Sweden was the policy of the individual parties. The Swedish Social Democratic Party was split on the issue, and an opinion poll showed that 40 Social Democratic MPs were against, and 20 in favour of membership. The Party consequently declared that membership in the EMU in 1999 was out of the question, a decision that was largely made with party unity in mind.[1]

The Swedish government's bill on the issue also reflects the divided opinions on the issue. While the Finnish government handled the issue as a statement procedure, where the role of the parliament was merely to express its opinion, the Swedish government submitted a bill to parliament (1997/98: 25) on 'Sweden and Economic and Monetary Union'. In its bill the government proposed that Sweden should not introduce the Euro when the third stage of EMU is started, but keep the door open for a later participation in the monetary union.[2]

---

[1] Pierre and Widfelt 1998, 528.

[2] Government bill 1997/98: 25.

There was not only a difference in how the issue was handled in Sweden and Finland, but also a difference in the attitudes towards membership. According to the Swedish government's bill

> ...participation in the monetary union must have a strong democratic basis..... After January 1, 1999, the government, if it finds that Sweden should participate in the monetary union, will submit the question to the Swedish people for consideration. It is desirable that such a test must be made in a general election, but an extra election or referendum instead cannot be ruled out. Thereafter it is for the Riksdag to take the final decision.[1]

The EMU debate in Sweden was characterised by a traditional Swedish policy making style with thorough consultation and deliberation.[2] Various information leaflets were published for businesses and households. A telephone service (Government Offices Euro information) was set up to answer questions about the Euro, and advertising campaigns in the media had been conducted. In addition, the issue was examined in a Commission of Enquiry before the government submitted its bill. The Commission's conclusion was that Sweden should 'wait and see', because in 1996 it was still not clear how the monetary union would develop. The government largely supported the Commission's conclusion.[3]

The vast information campaign in Sweden did not differ to any great extent from the Finnish one. Various advertising campaigns were also conducted in Finland, and information leaflets mailed to households and businesses. The prime minister appointed an expert group on 28.11.1996, with the task of evaluating the impact of the EMU on the Finnish economy. The group was to submit its report by May 1998. (This report also formed the basis for the statement report submitted to parliament.) In its report, the group pointed out various positive, as well as negative factors influencing the Finnish decision. The positive reasons were that the EMU would reduce interest rates, reduce costs caused by currency exchanges, reduce the need for protecting measures against currency fluctuations, increase internal European trade by the dissolution of currency fluctuations, and an improved comparability of prices between countries. According to the group, the financial advantages of membership would be significantly higher than the costs. The risks associated with membership would be

---

[1] Government bill 1997/98: 25.

[2] Anton 1969.

[3] Pierre and Widfelt 1997, 497.

related to whether Britain and Sweden joined the first wave, the weak financial public economy of some central countries in Europe, and the exchange fluctuations against the American dollar and Japanese yen. The Finnish government nonetheless regarded membership in the EMU as being the best means in achieving steady economic growth and a reduced unemployment.[1] Despite the fact that Sweden and Finland prepared the decision on whether to join the EMU in similar ways, the outcome was different since Finland decided to join, while Sweden stayed outside. In Finland, the issue was more or less forced through by a seemingly united government, whilst the Swedish government was divided on the issue and therefore decided to 'wait and see'.

Despite the fact that the main economic interest groups and the government heavily supported membership, the way the decision was made was heavily criticised by parties in opposition to the government. Compared to the working hours case from 1965, and the work reform case, it therefore seems relevant to argue that a consensus between the main economic interest groups and governments leaves little room for dissensus and opposition to have any impact.

Conclusions

Finnish labour market policy making has since 1944 been characterised by a regularised relationship between the main economic interest groups and governments, and it is relevant to say that elite accommodation has in several ways become institutionalised. There are also several features that would support a sectoral quasi-consociational model of interest intermediation. The regularised arrangements between the main economic interest groups and governments have enabled the development of a labour market characterised by broad-based incomes policy settlements, despite the fact that there are conflicting views among workers and employers on Finnish labour market.

A common feature of both the corporate pluralist and consociational models is therefore that they presuppose consensus. In corporatist models it is an (economic) consensus that emerges from the self-subordination of functional interest on the labour market to common goals, whilst the consociational models presuppose a (non-economic) consensus at the elite decision making level. Without an evaluation of the third level of

[1] Government statement report 20.5.1997, 18; 22-23; 50.

consensus (policy consensus), these broad categorisations remain rather superficial. If characterising Finnish labour market policy making as corporate pluralist, it basically does not add more to our knowledge and understanding of the issue than to say that the relationship between the main economic interest groups and governments has been regularised and close. Similarly, if characterising it as quasi-consociational, it basically does not add more to our knowledge and understanding of the issue than to say that consensual solutions have been found at the elite decision making level, despite the fact that there are conflicting views among workers and employers. The problem with such models becomes a question of whether they apply to countries as such, or whether prefixes have to be added in order to adopt them to, in this case, Finnish labour market. As noted in the previous chapter, this was the reason why corporatism lost most of its conceptual importance. To state that Finnish labour market policy making is a form of sectoral quasi-consociationalism would be a return to the same problems authors on corporatism faced, i.e. the difficulty to implement the concept as a whole. (This can also be regarded as a problem for the pluralist forms of interest intermediation.) The implementation of the concepts of corporate pluralism and quasi-consociationalism are therefore not suitable in analyses of specific policy making decisions. They are more suitable in comparative analyses of superstructures between different countries.

An analysis of the third level of consensus is required in order to reveal what it means in practice when consensus has, in many respects, been institutionalised, and whether it brings any side-effects. Based on evidence from the 1965 working hours case, the EMU and the work reform cases, it seems to be difficult to get alternative views accepted if there is a general consensus on the issues between the main economic interest groups and the government. The empirical analysis of the working hours case should provide for a more in-depth evaluation of what a Finnish model of institutionalised elite accommodation means in practice in the working hours case. By such an analysis, it should be possible to reveal something about current Finnish labour market policy making. Before going into the in-depth analysis, the next chapter will provide the necessary background information in order to be able to understand the problems faced by the participants in the committees that eventually built consensus on the issue.

4 Working Hours and Organised Interests – the Current Dilemma

The first aim of this chapter is to describe the current system of Finnish labour market regulations. It is of vital importance to know how the system works, since this is reflected in the positions of the different participants in the formulating process, which is analysed in the next chapter. The second aim is to take a scientific approach and show the importance of working hours in social research. This is shown by an overview of how the concept has been approached in economic and sociological research. The chapter concludes with an evaluation of the basic dilemmas the participants in the committee and working group are facing in trying to reach consensus on the issue.

It is no overstatement to say that working hours, together with wages, represent the central issues of disputes in the labour market. The recent debate has focused mainly on different models of working hour arrangements, since it has been regarded as fairly obvious, that too general and rigid models have failed to take into account the specific situations individual firms face. Too general models have also failed to take into account the skills of individual workers.[1] Prevailing and outdated working hour arrangements, together with current rates of economic growth, have been regarded as a hindrance to the creation of new jobs.[2] Requirements for new working hour arrangements in terms of when, and how, working hours are placed during the day, week and year have therefore been regarded as an important policy-measure in improving employment and economic efficiency.[3] The main objective has consequently been how to create greater opportunities for more individualised flexible arrangements. In Finland,

[1] Sarfati and Kobrin 1988, 31.

[2] Blyton 1985, 36-37.

[3] duRoy et al. 1989; McRae 1995; Bercusson and Dickens 1996; Taddei 1998.

this has to take place in the context of a thoroughly regulated labour market.

Finnish Working Hours Regulations

The regulations for the Finnish labour market are contained in a complex mixture of three categories: legislation, collective agreements and employment contracts. The complexity of the regulations is also underlined by the opportunities for making diverging statements from legislation at the collective agreements, local collective agreements, and individual agreements level. In addition, regulations included in broad-based incomes policy settlements have also sometimes demanded revisions of legislation, especially in the early 1970s.

Legislation

Legislation has been developed as a means of securing workers' rights and basic security. Examples of regulations by law in Finland are the holiday act, working hours act, act for protection at work, employment contracts act, co-operation act etc. All these acts basically contain a number of statutory obligations for employers and consequently statutory rights for workers.[1] These are, of course, enacted by parliament.

Collective Agreements

The second category, collective agreements, is the most important of Finnish labour market regulations. There are four different levels of collective agreements. The first level consists of broad-based incomes policy settlements, which are concluded at the national level between the central confederations of trade unions and employers' associations. The conclusion of these settlements has been supported by the government, which appoints the mediator who leads the negotiations. As mentioned earlier, these settlements contain extensive national economic policy measures, as well as expressed expectations on wages, agriculture, taxation etc. Working hours were not included in the settlements until 1986, when the parties agreed on a reduction of working hours. In 1989, a statement on

---

[1] Bruun 1998, 209.

the need for research on working hours was included, and in 1990 there was a statement on the need for setting up a working hours committee.

In legal terms, the trade unions and employers' associations are not formally required to comply with the broad based settlements, which have been agreed upon in negotiations between the central confederations of trade unions, the national employers' associations and supported by the government. They are, however, expected to do so. If some of the large trade unions, for example the Metal or Paperworkers' Unions, decide to seek after greater advantages than the broad-based settlement would allow, the whole settlement falls, and all sectors make their individual sectoral collective agreements. If the trade unions and employers' associations comply with the expectations in the broad-based settlements, the sectoral collective agreements are consequently based on these expectations. The broad-based settlements therefore form the framework for agreements made at the second level of collective agreements, i.e. sectoral collective agreements. (It is, however, also possible to conclude sectoral collective agreements without any broad-based settlement.) Agreements concluded at the sectoral level are comprehensive, as well as detailed, and form an important means in regulating the terms under which actual work is carried out in different sectors on the labour market.[1] A sectoral collective agreement can only be concluded between employers or employers' associations as one party and trade unions as the other. Another important feature of the sectoral collective agreements is that they are binding, not only for members of organisations who have signed the agreement, but also for individuals who work in similar sectors to the ones that have signed it. Thus, even if a worker is not a trade union member, his employer has to give him/her the same advantages as he gives to the ones who are trade union members. (This also refers to the principle of universal commitment, explained earlier.)

There is also a special relationship between the collective agreements and legislation. Whilst legislation has provided the general framework within which regulations for the labour market are to be arranged, it has in many cases been able to make diverging arrangements in collective agreements between the parties in the labour market. In the case of working hours, for example, individual workers and employers have had the opportunity to make arrangements, on for example, flexitime, length of daily rests and opportunities for translating overtime hours into extra free-time. The only exceptions where regulations in the working hours act are

[1] Bruun 1998, 211-212.

mandatory, are the definitions of extratime and overtime, agreement by workers to do extra- and overtime, maximum amount of working hours, and the employer's duty to write down the amount of working hours their workers complete. Diverging regulations in sectoral collective agreements have been possible on all other working hour issues.[1] Accordingly, working hours have for most workers in practice been regulated through various collective agreements, since, in all, around 95 per cent of workers and employers are bound by some form of collective agreements. The rest of the labour market (5 per cent) is the so-called wild, unorganised field *(villi kenttä)*, consisting of workers who work for unorganised employers not belonging to any employers' association, and not covered by the so-called universal commitment. An example of such a sector in Finland is hairdressing.

There is, furthermore, a great difference between sectors in the implementation of working hours regulations. For example, in the sectoral collective agreement for the metal industry, in force 1994-95, the starting point was that a conclusion of individual agreements on working hours at the workplace level was to be regarded as the primary objective. If the employers and their workers could not reach such agreements, then the sectoral collective agreement covering the whole sector was to be implemented.[2] In the sectoral collective agreement for the paper industry on the other hand, there were no opportunities for making individual agreements at the firm level. The sectoral, and nation-wide, regulations were to be implemented in all workplaces, i.e. same regulations for all.[3] The reason for this may be found in the basic structure of the metal and paper industry. The metal industry covers a wide range of usually small companies making different products, while the paper industry comprises of large companies who basically make one product; paper.

The third level of collective agreements is concluded at local levels in usually large companies, who are not members of any employers' association. Examples of such companies are the Finnish Broadcasting Company and the national airline Finnair. These agreements are concluded

---

[1] Similar arrangements have been adopted in Sweden where it, since 1982, has been possible to diverge from the entire working hours act by collective agreements. These agreements have had to be approved by the central confederations of trade unions and employers associations.

[2] Collective agreement for the metal industry 1994, 53-54.

[3] Collective agreement for the paper industry 1994, 16-41.

on the basis of specific delegatory provisions included in the sectoral collective agreements.

The fourth and final level of collective agreement regulations is agreements between individual employers and workers. The purpose of individual agreements is to agree on more advantageous terms than the collective agreements provide, since collective agreements define the minimum conditions that have to be implemented. Advantages granted by the collective agreements cannot be reduced by individual agreements.[1] The implementation of individual agreements has become, and is regarded as becoming more common in the future.

Employment Contracts

The third category of labour market regulations in Finland is employment contracts, regulated in the employment contracts act. These contracts are made between individual workers and employers. They usually state that workers are obliged to carry out work carefully and in accordance with their employer's instructions. The contracts also include other provisions that workers are obliged to fulfil such as to observe safety regulations and not to disclose business or industrial secrets. The employer's main obligation is to pay wages for the work performed.[2] There is also a specific relationship between employment contracts and the various forms of collective agreements. Whilst employment contracts are made without any time limits, collective agreements concern certain periods of time, usually two years. The employer must therefore ensure that the conditions set in the employment contract do not contradict the minimum conditions on wages, working hours, etc., set in collective agreements. If the employment contract contradicts the collective agreement, the regulations in the collective agreements rule, and the statements in the employment contract are invalid.[3] As mentioned in the introduction, another important part of the employment contract act is the principle of universal commitment.

The most important features of Finnish labour market regulations are therefore legislation, which forms the basic rights and obligations, broad-based incomes policy settlements, which outline the national economic and labour market policy; and sectoral collective agreements, which set out in detail what regulations are to be implemented in the different branches. It is

[1] Bruun 1998, 211.

[2] Bruun 1998, 208-209.

[3] Bruun 1998, 212.

also the relationship between these different regulations that pose a considerable dilemma in the working hours case. This is especially the case for the trade unions, but also for the employers' associations. This also sets the scene for a political analysis of working hours.

The Current Dilemma

Whilst the recent problem has become a requirement for more *flexibility*, as opposed to the same collective regulations for all, the early debate on working hours had been concerned mainly with the lengths of working hours. In the nineteenth century, demands for reduced working hours were often made by workers' representatives. They regarded shortened working hours as a means in creating a more even distribution of jobs among the whole working population. This job-sharing argument was presented in Great Britain in the late nineteenth century, in connection with demands for an eight-hour working day. It was brought forward again in the 1930s, when the economic depression resulted in demands for policy measures that could curb unemployment. More recent rises in unemployment during the 1970-80s also resulted in a return to the job-sharing argument. The argument was basically based on assumptions that the reduction of working hours would create a shortfall in labour supply, with the result that employers would have to hire more workers in order to maintain the same level of production.[1]

A related approach to the job-sharing argument as a means in creating jobs has been a lowering of retirement age and the increase of part-time retirement. The most common argument in favour of earlier retirement has been the productivity-factor. An increasing ill health, occupational inertia and a growing inability to accept and integrate new work methods have been seen as the main reasons behind a decline in productivity. Arguments expressed in favour of lower retirement ages as a mean in creating jobs have been that the type of workers most likely to retire early would be the ones with a relatively low occupational status. Since the unemployed often are dominated by low- or unskilled younger workers, the occupational structure of the early retiring workers would match the occupational structure of the unemployed.[2]

---

[1] Blyton 1985, 35-36.

[2] Hart 1987, 233, 239.

Reduced working hours as a means of creating more jobs, may for laypersons, be regarded as a simple and effective policy. In economic research, where different kind of econometric models are usually applied the relationship between reduced working hours and job-creation has not been that straightforward. The job-sharing argument, for example, has on the one hand been seen as based on the false premise of labour as a constant entity, where the economy is supposed to demand a specific amount of labour in a static economy. Job-sharing as an important instrument in improving employment, has therefore been regarded as rather limited. Micro-economic studies of work-places have on the other hand showed that reduced working hours could increase employment at one work place, but that does not automatically mean that it applies to all workplaces. It rather depends on the political, social, and economic context, and at the same time, whether the economy as a whole has an excess supply of labour.[1] The basic difficulty with questions on whether reduced working hours also create employment, has therefore been that an implementation of this policy usually has failed to take into account underlying labour market relationships. These relationships have been seen in terms of different constraints, for example maximum amounts of overtime and overtime compensation imposed by legislation, as well as the effects of collective agreements on simplified and idealised econometric models of working hours. Shorter working hours may according to economic research produce employment benefits if, and only if, some kind of increased productivity, wage restraints or selective subsidies are implemented at the same time. Otherwise reductions in working hours may have the opposite effect, that is, have no effect on the creation of employment, or even lead to higher unemployment.[2]

Despite the theoretical risks in adopting these working hour policies, they have been widely implemented in Europe. A Job Release Scheme was established by the government in Great Britain in 1977, which enabled workers to take early retirement before reaching the statutory retirement age, on condition that someone else was employed in their place. A new law in West Germany in 1984, enabled workers to retire at the age of 58, and the state paid 35 per cent of the early retirement pension if the employer replaced the retired by an unemployed person.[3] More recently, as noted in the introduction, the *loi Aubry* in France set the regular weekly

---

[1] Cuvillier 1984, 104, 141-142; Rubin and Richardson 1997, 134.

[2] Hart 1987, 126-127; 269.

[3] Sarfati and Kobrin 1988, 29.

amount of working hours in medium sized and large companies from 39 hours to 35 by January 2000, and in companies with less than 20 employees by January 2002. The 35-hour working week policy was first introduced in the 1997 election campaign by Lionel Jospin, who was the leader of the Socialist Party, as a means of cutting unemployment. After Jospin became the new prime minister in France after the election, the 35-hour working week was made into law.

In Finland, three special schemes have been implemented during the 1990s – a job-rotation scheme, a part-time supplement scheme, and a 6+6 hour day shift scheme. The job-rotation scheme was intended for workers who wanted to take temporary time off for study, or family reasons, while at the same time another person was given the job temporarily. The scheme was based on voluntary agreements between the workers and employers. Under the part-time supplement scheme, in force between 1994-96, a person who voluntarily changed from full-time to part-time could be granted a supplementary payment to compensate for the loss of earnings. The employer then had to recruit an unemployed person for the period the ordinary worker worked part-time. The six+six scheme meant that work was organised in two six-hour shifts, without a one-hour lunch break. The model was therefore meant to enhance productivity at the same time as it improved employment. The implementation of these schemes has remained at a low level, however.[1]

Whilst working hours have been regarded as an important factor in creating jobs, they have, from a sociological point of view, been regarded as a dependent variable of more overall social changes in society. Labour was in the nineteenth century regarded as distinct from other social activities, like for example family life. The chief organising principle of social structures was the position of workers in the production process, and social development was seen as originating in conflicts between workers and owners of industrial enterprises.[2] Modern social science has challenged these traditional features, a challenge, which has stressed a crisis of the employment society, where work no longer should be seen as the most important cornerstone in society. According to one sociological approach, a standardised concept of work is no longer possible. The reasons for this are based on a growing difference between work in manufacturing and service, as well as an overall individualisation of work environments through the increasing use of agreements between workers and employers at the

[1] Labour market studies, Finland, 1996, 56-57.

[2] Offe 1985, 132-134.

workplace level. Employment based on salaried work is therefore no longer to serve as the basic starting point for organisational or political behaviour, since membership in social classes is no longer to be seen as a determining factor in shaping the conduct of life. The new structures of society have instead been viewed in terms of a transition from a paradigm of distribution, to a paradigm of forms of life. Contemporary social and political conflicts are according to this approach therefore no longer to be derived from capital versus labour, but to be seen as deriving from dichotomies of materialism vs. post-materialism, and industrial production versus household work.[1] From this sociological approach, our society is thus supposed to have reached the end of the employment era when work has become less central compared with other aspects of social life.

These perceptions of the current labour market and society may be somewhat exaggerated. While the individualisation tendencies have led to a non-standardisation of work, there is little evidence that work as a central feature of contemporary societies is on the decline, simply ask the views of the unemployed. Unemployment still represents a significant social stigma where loss of work strongly interferes with a deeply ingrained desire to obtain paid work in society.[2] While the character of work may be changing, the importance of work in society is still central as a crucial part of the capitalist consumption society.

Regardless of whether focus is on economic or sociological approaches to working hours, the overall current debate in the 1990s has been focusing on, as noted above, how to create a more flexible labour market.[3] For both workers and employers, the new working hours policy has therefore been directed towards the creation of flexible arrangements, suitable for individual options, when traditional working hours policy has been directed towards general, universal working hour arrangements,

---

[1] Offe 1985, 149-150.

[2] Little 1985, 278.

[3] Flexibility may be seen as a recent phenomenon of the 1990s, but the Organisation for Economic Co-operation and Development (OECD) had already started to discuss new patterns for working hour arrangements in the mid 1960s. The problem was seen as how to introduce greater flexibility in the allocation of working hours, such as flexibility of retirement age, education and training during working-life, part-time work and temporary employment. (OECD 1973, 6) The issue of flexible working hours has stayed on the agenda within OECD, when its recent research has been focusing on empirical evaluations of how flexibility has been applied on the labour markets in Europe. (OECD 1986; 1990; 1992; 1995.)

equally binding to all.[1] Workers' demands for new arrangements can be seen as a result of at least three different reasons. The first one is the increasing participation by women on the labour market. The traditional pattern of full-time, lifetime employment has been seen as a male model where women were supposed to take care of the household work. In a post-industrial society, this model is no longer supposed to represents the actual circumstances on the labour market. A reduction in the numbers of full-time, lifetime housewives has called for the demand for more flexible and individualised working hour arrangements. Workers are seen as entering the labour market with special demands for individual arrangements because of family situations etc.[2] The second reason is demands by an increasing number of people combining education with work, and the third reason increasingly diverse lifestyles.

For the employers, the demands for new working hour arrangements still to some extent correlate with the reasons why working hours were increased in the early industrialisation era, i.e. in order to enhance production. Employers' requirements for flexible working hour arrangements in the 1990s have been the needs for extending operating hours in order to make better use of their existing capital and to be able to adjust working hours according to fluctuations in orders.[3] Although both employers and workers favour more flexible arrangements, their interests do not necessarily coincide. Employers' demands for extended operating hours, usually implying unattractive time arrangements for workers, may not correlate with workers' demands for individualised personal arrangements, coupled with demands for a collective security. The needs for new working hour arrangements in Finland have therefore put special demands on the traditional bargaining patterns, where collective agreements have played an important role. (This problem was also clearly visible in the Centre party's Work reform, described in the previous chapter.)

From a sociological point of view, working hours have therefore been regarded as a dependent variable, explained by the changes in the overall structure of society and labour markets. From an economic research point of view, working hours have been regarded an independent variable, explaining, for example, reduced unemployment. Working hours as a research problem in political science is, of course, different from these

[1] Hörning et al. 1995, 28-29.

[2] Hewitt, 1993, 4-6; OECD 1995, 11; McRae 1995.

[3] OECD 1995, 9-38.

approaches. That does not mean, however, that the sociological and economic views of the problem are irrelevant from a political science point of view. They set the contextual framework within which the political analysis takes place. The problem of developing new working hours regulations stems from both the sociological view of a changing society and labour market, and the economists' view of needs for changing working hour arrangements to improve economic efficiency. As noted earlier, regulations on working hours since 1944 have mainly been made by different kinds of collective agreements between the parties on the labour market. The objective and dilemma for the committee that prepared the new working hours act, was to include opportunities for more individualised and firm level agreements into legislation. It would therefore indicate a shift away from the corporate pluralist era, since opportunities for individual and flexible arrangements could be agreed upon according to legislation. The importance of the general agreements between the main economic interest groups, as well as collective working hour arrangements between the national trade unions and employers' associations would therefore be reduced.

Conclusions

With these background features in mind, it is possible to more exactly outline the basic preferences of employers and trade unions. The main objective for employers has been to increase the opportunity for flexible agreements through legislation, without the opportunity to make delegatory statements in collective agreements. This would in turn reduce some of the power of the national trade unions and employers' associations in favour of individual employers. This would also create greater demands on shop stewards, since they would increasingly have to negotiate directly with the employer. The employers' basic standpoint has consequently been a favouring of mandatory statements in legislation, which cannot be delegated to collective agreements. Their standpoint therefore also relates to the problem of working hours as an independent variable in enhancing economic efficiency. *The main dilemma for the employers has therefore become how to extend the operating hours of business, within the limits set by government regulations and collective agreements.*[1]

---

[1] OECD 1995, 13.

The issue is more of a dilemma for the trade unions. At the same time as the workforce is concerned with more individualised working hour arrangements to balance time spent between work and spare-time, the trade unions also have to be able to defend their members' interests collectively.[1] *The dilemma for the trade unions is consequently how to combine the current trend of demands for individual flexible labour market regulations with the collective security of workers.* The European Trade Union Confederation (ETUC) have stated that more flexible and individualised working hour arrangements can be accepted only if they are at the same time subjected to collective negotiations. The dilemma for the trade unions therefore relates more to the sociological problem of working hours as depending on a changing labour market. A special focus in the case study that follows in the next chapter will therefore be on how the workers' representatives dealt with this problem. The problem for the chairperson is how to mediate between the employers' and workers' representatives and propose legally acceptable statements that both sides can accept.

The next chapter will therefore focus on a political approach to the working hours issue. The case study represents an analysis of how the objective of introducing opportunities for more flexible arrangements according to legislation was achieved; how the different parties taking part influenced the outcome; what arguments they expressed during the decision making process; how consensus was reached on the issue; and finally, how dissent, dissensus and opposition was dealt with. (A new act was approved by the parliament in 1996.)

[1] OECD 1995, 12.

5 The Formulation of Working Hours Legislation – Corporate Pluralist Deliberation as Consensus Building?

As has been reiterated earlier in this thesis there are several features of contemporary Finnish politics and policy making that would imply consensus at the basic and procedural levels, i.e. consensus over common goals in society and how conflicts are resolved. The first aim of this chapter is to focus on the third dimension of consensus, i.e. the policy level. The chapter concentrates on how the working hours issue was discussed and decided, how dissensus and opposition was treated, and how consensus on the issue was eventually reached.

The second aim of this chapter is to evaluate whether the corporate pluralist arrangements constitute a good form of policy making by reference to the working hours case. People differ, of course, in their perceptions of what is a good policy. For example, as noted in the previous chapter the employers' representatives in Finland regard flexible and individualised agreements on working hours as good, while the workers' representatives regard sectoral collective agreements as good. The aim is not, however, to make any judgement of which of these views are more preferable, but focus on the decision making process itself, and whether it itself can be characterised as good. The normative justification of the participation of the main economic interest groups in labour market policy making was based on their possession of relevant knowledge of labour market conditions. When analysing specific decision making processes, such broad concepts become difficult to operationalise, and further qualifications are required. A useful operationalisation as to determining whether the procedure has been good can be found in the normative discussions on democracies, where political arrangements tie the exercise of power to free reasoning among equals. The objective in this chapter is therefore to evaluate whether the process has been characterised by participants who have been free from external constraints; equal in the sense that none of them have gained special advantages or disadvantages; and reasonable in their arguments in that they have defended them in a way that others have a reason to accept.[1] If these criteria have been met, and the result is consensus on the issue, then the process can be regarded as good.

The situation in Finland at the beginning of the 1990s was one of crisis. A gradual deregulation of the obstacles in the way of borrowing foreign capital in the mid to late 1980s had led to an exceptional boom and growth in the economy. The 'spending fiest' *(kulutusjuhla)* was at its highest at the end of the 1980s and early 1990s, leading to a rapid growth of borrowing and money supply. The economy was overheating and the Finnish foreign debt became a problem. At a meeting of the Economic Council in March 1989, experts warned that unless something was done about the foreign debt, a growing inflation, higher interest rates and large unemployment would follow in the 1990s.[2] After the parliamentary election in 1991, the subsequent centre-right wing government, led by the Centre Party together with the Conservatives, continued the hard-currency approach the previous government had advocated.[3] The experts' warnings proved to be accurate, albeit that they could not have predicted the severity of the situation, caused by the collapse of the Soviet Union in 1990.

Finland was hit by a serious economic recession and mass unemployment, which rose from a negligible 3.5 per cent in 1990, to over 20 per cent in 1993. An overvaluation of the Finnish currency and a declining industrial competitiveness resulted in a devaluation of the currency by 12.3 per cent in 1991. The efforts did not protect the currency from further speculations, and the Bank of Finland was forced to allow the currency to float in 1992. The value of the Finnish stock-market collapsed and the banking system had to be supported by state funding in order to prevent it from bankruptcy. As a consequence, higher taxation was imposed, together with lay-off of employees in every section of the labour

---

[1] Cohen 1989, 22-23.

[2] Aho 1998, 144-145.

[3] After Sweden made a surprising decision on the European Exchange Rate Mechanism in May 1991, Finland was according to the prime minister left with three options: follow suit, revise a previous decision to revaluate the currency from 1989, or devaluate. (Aho 1998, 149) At the proposal by the Bank of Finland, the Finnish currency was bound to the European Exchange Rate Mechanism in 1991.

market. The labour market was not only hit by mass unemployment, but the people who remained at work also faced a new situation of increasing insecurity with threats of further lay-offs.

All the main economic interest groups and the government agreed that some revisions of labour market regulations had to be made in order to solve some of the problems that the labour market had started to face in the 1990s. Arguments for such changes were mostly voiced by the employers. They had, throughout the 1980s, argued for a more de-regularised and flexible labour market in order to improve productivity. According to them, the traditional system of regulating the labour market by collective agreements between trade unions and employers associations, had become too rigid and inflexible, unable to take into account the needs of individual companies and branches.[1] As mentioned in the previous chapter, for the trade unions, the problems on the labour market posed a considerable dilemma. On the one hand they had to take into account the productivity and competitivenes of companies, and therefore refrain from too great demands on pay rises and other benefits which could possibly have created further bankruptcies and lay-offs. On the other hand, they also had to preserve the collective rights and strengths of workers, since they could not leave all issues to be dealt with between individual employers and workers. Employers consequently demanded new and extensive policy measures in order to make the labour market regulations more flexible, which opposed traditional demands by trade unions to preserve and secure the collective rights of workers.

Before the economic recession set in, the need for a revision of the working hours legislation was seen as an important measure in the development of labour market regulations. Included in the broad-based settlement for 1990-91 were therefore urgent demands for appointing a committee to prepare and discuss the matter. This committee was to be set up on a tripartite basis with members of the central confederations of trade unions, national employers' associations and independent experts. The committee should evaluate the scope for a reduction in the great number of working hours regulations, evaluate opportunities for more flexible and individualised working hours to be regulated at the firm level, as well as evaluate other deficiencies in the current working hours legislation. The government consequently appointed an ad hoc working hours committee on a tripartite basis. The committee started its work in 1990, and had to present its report by February 28, 1993.

---

[1] Committee proposal 1992: 39, 49.

The Working Hours Committee

The analysis of the case has been based on arguments stated by parties from different stages of the decision making process, i.e. before the process began in 1990, during the committee's work 1990-93 and the aftermath of its work 1993-95. The material used for the analysis consisted mainly of written unofficial documents and comments, statements written down by the chairperson, unofficial and official memoranda, faxmessages by the parties and discussions with the negotiators. Based on this material, the working hours issue could be divided into three different issue categories: unanimity, compromise and conflict. The unanimous issues were characterised by a lack of discussion, since the parties did not comment on the content of them. These issues did not touch upon the parties' preferences, since many of them were merely of legalistic nature that had to be included in all legislation. There were in all eight such issues: (the numbers in the brackets refers to the committee's proposal for paragraph number in the new act).

1. Who has the authority to settle conflicts over range of application (§3).
2. The changes in day and week according to the calendar week and year (§13).
3. Rights to derogate from obligation to make lists on shift-work (§32).
4. The period within which an appeal may be lodged against the act (§34).
5. The employers' duty to keep the working hours act visible at all workplaces (§36).
6. The supervision that the act is correctly implemented (§38).
7. The authority to state by decree otherwise than the act states (§39).
8. A decision by the government on how to arrange the start and finish of transport work at nights (§40).

The second category, i.e. issues of compromise, was more interesting, since these issues to a greater extent touched upon the different parties' preferences. These issues were resolved according to a form of legal reasoning, meaning that different types of solutions were compared in terms of similarities and differences.[1] This meant that the chairperson made a proposal for a new paragraph, which was then discussed in the committee. Based on this discussion, the chairperson made revised proposals, and eventually all the parties could accept a final proposal.

[1] March and Olsen 1989.

These issues naturally implied action in terms of the calculation of the options available and their possible consequences, but they could to a greater extent be characterised as argumentation in favour of, or against, certain statements. If a new act had been based on these issues alone, a revised working hours act would have caused no problems, since the parties reached an agreement on them. There were in all 28 such issues:

1. The range of application of the act (§1).
2. Exemptions to § 1 (§2).
3. The definition of working hours (§4).
4. The time when an employee must be at his employer's disposal (§5).
5. The arrangements of derogatory working hours and maximum length of working hours over two and three week periods (§7).
6. The definition of flexi-time (§9).
7. Regular working hours based on collective agreements (§10).
8. The derogations from regular working hours by the Council of Occupational Safety and Health (§11).
9. Shortened working hours (§12).
10. Extra and overtime work (§14).
11. The approval by the employee to work extra- and overtime (§15).
12. How to arrange beginning and ending of working hours in order to get continuance between shifts (§17).
13. The definition of emergency work (§18).
14. The wage for extra and overtime work (§20).
15. The calculation of basic salary for extra and overtime work (§22).
16. Nightwork (§23).
17. The maximum amount of nightshifts in period work (§24).
18. The definition of daily rest periods (§25).
19. The definition of 24-hour rest periods (§26).
20. The definition of weekly rest periods (§27).
21. Derogations from weekly rest periods (§28).
22. Sunday work (§29).
23. How to equalise working hours that are counted over a specific period (§30).
24. The lists of shift work (§31).
25. Book-keeping of working hours (§33).
26. The mandatory status of the working hours act (§35).
27. Statutes on punishment (§37).
28. Statutes on commencement of the act (§41).

Finally, there were five issues in the category of conflict:

1. A general statement about regular amounts of working hours (§6).
2. Regular working hours based on agreements at firm level (§8).
3. The maximum amount of overtime work (§16).
4. Wage for extra and overtime work (§19).
5. The ending of employment contract during period when working hours are equalised (§21).

All but the final one (§21) of these five issues of conflict dealt to some extent with opportunities for introducing agreements on working hours at firm level, as a complement to the traditional way of making the agreements according to the sectoral collective agreements.[1] The specific content of the conflict on collective agreements versus agreements at firm levels concerned opportunities for making agreements at the firm level on regular amount of working hours, and on maximum amount of overtime (§§6, 8 and 16). Traditionally, such opportunities had been possible only under the auspices of the national trade unions and employers associations according to §10, quoted earlier in chapter two. The statement gave the trade unions and employers' associations rights to make their own collective agreements on working hours, with the same status as legislation.[2] (The basic relationship between these collective agreements and other forms of regulations in Finland was explained in chapter three.)

The content of the last issue of conflict (§19), was a complicated detail concerned with how payment was to be made during a period when sectoral collective agreements had ended, and no new ones had still been agreed upon. This conflict was basically on whether the employers had a right to reduce the salary if the period that had ended did not come up to a total of 40 hours. The employers' representative regarded this paragraph as unnecessary, while the workers' representatives were more or less satisfied with the proposal by the chairperson.[3] Despite it being a question of explicit

[1] The traditional way of making agreements was preserved in the section on regular working hours based on collective agreements (§10). The conflicts concerned exemptions from that paragraph.

[2] A similar statement has also been included into the Swedish working hours act. In the proposal for a revision of the Swedish act it was explicitly stated that questions around working hours should as far as possible be made by collective agreements where legislation only should serve as basic security. (SOU 1996, 145, 155.)

[3] Memorandum by TT 15.4.1993, Committee proposal 1993: 2 (appendix 2), 8-9.

conflict when the chairperson suggested two alternatives in the committee's proposal, the issue was nonetheless of minor importance, since the employers' representatives were unconvinced that the paragraph was needed at all. The main conflicts in the committee consequently dealt with issues concerning how negotiations on working hours issues were to be arranged in the future - according to agreements at a national level or extended opportunities for agreements at the firm level. The conflict, therefore, not surprisingly related to the basic preferences of employers, i.e. individual flexible arrangements, as well as the basic dilemma for trade unions, i.e. how to preserve the collective rights of workers in the search for more flexibility. The focus will therefore be on how this problematic issue of the relationship between collective agreements and firm level agreements was resolved.

Agreements at Firm Level Based on Legislation

Before the committee started its work, all parties were in favour in one way or another of increasing opportunities for making firm level agreements. A central feature of statements made by the workers' representatives before the committee started its work, was that the individual and personal opinions of workers had to be taken into account. This was clearly expressed in a memorandum from 1990, when the largest confederation of trade unions (SAK), outlined the basic principles for the development of working hours legislation. In these principles, the importance of collective agreements was secondary to the importance of individual workers needs.

> The starting point is not only a reduction of working hours, but also that the personal and individual needs of employees have to be taken into account. In making agreements on working hours, the employee has to be able independently to choose the kind of working hours that suits him best.[1]
>
> If opportunities for agreements at firm level are included into the working hours legislation, the trade unions must have the possibility to supervise the procedures. The law must also include a basic right for workers that cannot be overlooked, not even by national collective agreements.[2]

This was also in line with the employers' view of the needs for development.

---

[1] Työaikaselonteko 1991, 30.

[2] Työaikaselonteko 1991, 33.

> The current view of working hours is still characterised by a sense of collective rigidness. We need more educated and experienced workers ... who can work in a responsible way in situations demanding flexibility and versatility.[1]

The employers' representatives also stressed that a labour market policy based on agreements at the firm level was important, since it would improve the competitiveness of companies and create more responsible workers. Both parties thus stressed the needs of individual workers and employers.

It was significant for the statements during the committee's work that the workers' representatives still held that some changes in the working hours legislation were necessary in the difficult economic period that Finland faced at that time. According to them, merely cosmetic changes were not enough, but if these changes were part of the collective agreements, they were willing to accept extended agreements at firm levels. In the view of the employers' representatives, the question of agreements at firm levels on working hours was most important. If such agreements were not included in the law, a revision was seen by them as unnecessary. During the process, the parties consolidated their own positions: the workers' representatives committed themselves to collective agreements and the employers to agreements at the firm level. According to the workers representatives '...[an introduction of opportunities for making agreements at the firm level] means a radical shift in the balance of negotiations'.[2]According to the employer's representatives '...this is the most important issue; agreements at the firm level must be developed'.[3]

The main divergence of interests could therefore be seen as a question of institutional choice, i.e. regulations in the form of collective agreements, as represented by trade unions, and in the form of individual agreements, as represented by employers' associations. The workers' representatives opposed the introduction of opportunities to make regulations on working hours according to legislation at the firm level, mainly because it would have changed a situation where trade unions had a form of veto-power to make binding agreements. The employers' position on the issue was the opposite, since opportunities for making agreements on working hours according to legislation would have reduced the power of trade unions.

[1] Memorandum 18.12.1989, 2.

[2] SAK 9.10.1992.

[3] TT 28.2.1992.

This would have provided employers with more freedom to implement flexible working hours simply by keeping within the framework provided by legislation, without having to resort to negotiations with the trade unions.

After the committee's work, the workers' representatives stressed that the central confederations of trade unions have the best opportunity of estimating the bargaining positions of the workers and of the employers.[1] And furthermore.

> In this deep recession, there is no need for a revision of the working hours act. Agreements made at the firm level must be developed in accordance with collective agreements.[2]

> The greatest deficiency in the committee's work is that the opportunity for trade union supervision of workers is weakened. It is surprising that alternatives are presented that do not take into account the rights of trade unions to make agreements. According to SAK, the economic recession and the spirit of time [i.e. a deregulated labour market] cannot be regarded as reasons for a revision of the act.[3]

In the employers' views, the committee had not brought forward any arguments that would speak against the need for agreements at firm levels, at the cost of collective agreements. According to them '...if [the alternative of agreements at firm levels] cannot be agreed upon according to legislation, there is no need for a new act at all'.[4]

Another main conflict in the working hours committee that touched upon opportunities for making agreements at firm levels, was the question of overtime. All parties in the committee made their own proposals for a maximum amount of overtime. In addition, the chairperson made two different proposals during the committee's work. According to his first proposal the maximum amount should be set at 52 hours over a four-week period, with an annual total amount of 320 hours.[5] The workers' representatives would have accepted this alternative. Their justification was that in an international perspective, the maximum amount of overtime was higher in Finland and therefore needed to be reduced. The employers'

---

[1] Committee proposal 1993: 2, 8.

[2] Memorandum of 15.4.1993, 4.

[3] Memorandum 15.4.1993, 4.

[4] TT 4.12.1992.

[5] Committee proposal 1993: 2, 143.

representatives could not accept this alternative. They justified their view by stating that the annual amount of working hours in Finland had been reduced by 300 hours since the previous legislative statement on working hours was made in 1966, which consequently would, according to them, mean that the annual amount of allowed overtime should be increased.[1]

In his second alternative, the chairperson proposed that the maximum amount of overtime be 72 hours over a four-week period. The annual total amount should be 320 hours, including an extra 160 hours that could be added according to agreements made at the firm level.[2] The employers' representatives would have accepted this proposal. The workers' representatives rejected opportunities for agreeing on extra overtime at the firm level, and thus rejected the second alternative.[3] As a result the committee's proposal on the issue of overtime was not unanimous when it presented two different alternatives in its report.

It is consequently fairly obvious that the problems for the committee to reach a final decision was caused by the basic standpoints of the parties, explained in the previous chapter. The employers' representatives would have approved of the chairperson's proposals since they correlated with their basic preference, i.e. how to extend operating hours of business. The workers' representatives rejected the proposal since it did not fit into their basic preferences of a stress of collective agreements.

The problematic character of extended opportunities for making agreements at firm levels can be further enlightened by looking at two other committees that had been appointed in 1992, and also consisted of representatives of the central confederations of trade unions and employers' associations. The *unofficial* comments on these committees' work, give additional information on how the employers' and workers' representatives dealt with the issue of extended opportunities for making agreements at the firm level. The explicit task of the first committee was to discuss and develop more flexible arrangements on the labour market in order to improve employment and the productivity of companies. This committee did not deal with working hours per se, but with an overall picture of the negotiation mechanisms on the labour market. The objective of the second committee was to revise and develop the annual holiday act, an issue that also had been included in the broad-based incomes policy settlement for 1990-91.

---

[1] Committee proposal 1993: 2 (appendix 2), 7-8.

[2] Committee proposal 1993: 2, 143.

[3] Memorandum by employers' association 15.4.1993, 2.

The Committee for developing negotiation mechanisms for the labour market Before this committee started its work, the aim of the workers' representatives in the committee was to make it possible for workers to conclude individual agreements with their employers on issues important for the workers. Such issues could be, for example, the content of work and equality at the workplace.[1] According to the employers' representatives an introduction of opportunities for flexible agreements was necessary, since it would make agreements between individual workers and employers possible, which in turn would have positive effects on profitability of companies. In addition, it would create a sense of responsibility for workers to increase their productivity as they could benefit from it more directly through individual agreements with their employers.[2]

During the committee's work, the different parties argued for their respective views on suggestions by the chairperson for the committee's proposal. According to the workers' representatives, the following sentences had to be *deleted* from the text written by the chairperson.[3]

> the present negotiation system is too rigid and reacts too late and slowly to changes.
>
> Since the workers and their personal needs are known at the work place, it is clear that the sense of responsibility is good enough at the firm level. Negotiations and agreements at firm levels on these questions probably lead to better and more equitable results than general norms.
>
> Agreements on a firm level would most probably lead to individual equality and enhanced profitability in salaries.

The employers' representatives made the following statements on the proposal by the chairperson.

> The statement that the workers are generally the weaker party at the firm level must be deleted. Instead it must be mentioned that individual freedom has been increased and workers' higher level of education makes firm level agreements more possible these days.[4]

---

[1] Memorandum by the chairperson January 28, 1993, 2.

[2] Committee proposal 1992: 39, 108.

[3] Fax message September 3, 1993.

[4] Fax message of August 20, 1993, 1-2.

> ...the conclusion must be, that collective agreements are to be transferred to the firm level, where it is possible to react quickly to changes.[1]

> The text must clearly state that the experiences of firm level agreements are always positive and strong developments are needed.[2]

> The text must clearly state that the general trend on the labour market is going toward a direction of firm level agreements.[3]

> The last sentence must be deleted since the examples presented there give a bad picture of agreements at the firm level.[4]

These statements indicated how the parties in the decision making process had an impact on the final result. Facts and statements by the independent chairperson that gave one party an advantage, had according to the other party to be deleted from the text. It was not the situation on the labour market in the eyes of the independent expert that was most important, but the image of the labour market in the eyes of the different parties.

After the committee had finished its work, the workers' representatives rejected the chairperson's suggestions. They took an entrenched stand on the issue and were not willing to discuss it further. Their strategy was to question the relevance of the statement and to refer to insufficiencies of legal-technical character. According to them, the proposal was not in line with the required standards that had to be met in law-drafting.[5] Furthermore, according to the workers' representatives, the committee's proposal was a sign of the times, since collective agreements had become regarded as a threat against economic development and had to be changed. They also claimed that the committee's proposal gave a totally erroneous picture of the contemporary system where collective agreements played the most central role. By sidestepping collective agreements and their social function, the committee did not take into account the shift in power this would mean. The views of the workers' representatives was that the negotiation mechanisms had to be revised according to a long-term

---

[1] Fax message of August 16, 1993, 1.
[2] Fax message of August 18, 1993, 1.
[3] Fax message of August 18, 1993, 1.
[4] Fax message of August 23, 1993, 1.
[5] Committee proposal 1993: 11 (appendix 2), 6.

perspective and not according to short-term economic prognoses. The national trade unions were to be seen as the major factor in developing the Nordic welfare state also in the future.[1]

In addition, the workers' representatives questioned the explanatory notes for the proposal, when the chairperson suggested opportunities of deviations from inflexible statements in the sectoral collective agreements. According to the workers' representatives, the sectoral collective agreements were approved by the national trade unions and employers' associations. Agreements that were not suitable for the labour market had to be adjusted by the trade unions and employers' associations – not by state intervention in the form of laws.[2] In other words, they justified their opinion by allowing for individual arrangements, but under the institutionalised system of making arrangements according to collective agreements.

> Firm level agreements must be developed according to the traditional procedure of making agreements.[3]

It is obvious that some of the proposals made by the independent chairperson, who was a professor at a university, did not fit into the preferences of the other parties. His statements that clashed with their interests had either to be deleted, or rewritten according to their preferences. It was therefore more of a maintenance of interests, than a seeking after consensus that decided the course of events. The problem of firm-level agreements was not only a problem in the committee for developing the negotiation mechanisms for the labour market, but also in the so-called annual holiday committee that dealt with a revision of the annual holiday act.

The annual holiday committee In the same broad-based incomes policy settlement where the requirements for a working hours committee was put forward, there was also a separate mention of the needs for a revision of the annual holiday act. The first annual holiday act had been enacted in 1919, and revised in 1946, 1973, 1978 and 1986. The objective of the committee was to reduce the possibilities for conflicting interpretations of the act that had occurred over the years, and to enable individual workers and

---

[1] Memorandum of 16.1.1993, 1-2.

[2] Committee proposal 1993: 11 (appendix 2), 10.

[3] Memorandum 16.1.1993, 1-2.

employers to be better able to judge their own rights and obligations, without having to consult legal expertise.[1]

The most problematic issue in this committee was how to define the annual holiday period. According to the workers' representatives, the normal period for taking annual holidays should be between June 1, and August 31. In addition, parents of small children should have the freedom to take some of the annual holiday during wintertime.[2] According to the employers' representatives, the system should be more flexible since the period from June 1 to August 31 was, for some branches, the most profitable months of the year. They furthermore thought that the annual holiday act should enable individual workers and employers to make individual agreements on when to have the annual holiday.[3] The workers' representatives heavily objected to the possibility of making agreements on annual holidays at the firm level. The reason for this was that it would, according to them, put the workers' representatives in firms under too heavy pressure. The workers' representatives in the committee could therefore 'under no circumstances' accept derogations from the sectoral collective agreements on when the annual holiday was to be held.[4]

The final proposal by the annual holiday committee did not lead to any changes in the holiday act because of disagreement between the parties on the issue. Returning to the working hours committee, it is therefore not very surprising, bearing in mind the two committees above, that its proposal was not unanimous. The main reason for this was the complete disagreement between the parties on the issue of opportunities for agreements made at firm levels.

The underlying feature of corporate pluralist arrangements is therefore not necessarily consensual in character. This does not mean, however, that the working hours case has to constitute a bad decision making process. If a good decision making process was characterised by free, equal and reasonable participants, a bad process would logically have meant non-free, unequal and unreasonable participants. The question of whether the participants were free from external constraints is interesting from an institutional point of view. As mentioned in chapter two, from a normative institutional perspective, institutions were important since they were regarded as defining the duties and obligations of a role in a specific

[1] Incomes policy settlement 30.11.1989, 10; Committee proposal 1993: 8, 192-193.

[2] Committee proposal 1993: 8, 179.

[3] Committee proposal 1993: 8, 179; Press release 3.3.1993, 1.

[4] Committee proposal 1993: 8, 197.

situation. If focusing on the workers' representatives, the definition of the duty and obligation was made by the main economic interest group. If, for some reason, some of them hold a different personal view, that person would consequently not have been free from external constraints. This is, of course, only a hypothetical assumption, but in a corporate pluralist context, where individuals act as representatives for organisations, it nonetheless shows the problems in determining whether someone has been free or not in their behaviour. It consequently also makes discussions of a good polity problematic. The issue of equality is more straightforward. The participants were equal in the sense that none of them have gained special advantages or disadvantages in the process. They were also reasonable in their arguments in that they defended them in a way that others had a reason to accept, since the counterparts knew their positions. Although the processes did not lead to consensus, it was not necessarily a bad decision making process.

The Aftermath of the Working Hours Committee's Work

In 1993, the working hours committee had not yet made any unanimous proposal for a revised working hours act. It became a task for the government, in particular the minister of labour, to try and find a solution to the problems in order to enable a submission of a government bill to the parliament. The government subsequently prepared a bill on a new working hours act to be submitted to the parliament in 1993. The bill was nonetheless withdrawn, because of the overall political and labour market situation in 1993.

During the turbulent economic climate in 1991, negotiations were also held for a broad-based incomes policy settlement for 1991-92, led by the former long-time Social Democratic prime minister Kalevi Sorsa. (At the 1991 parliamentary election, the Social Democrats lost eight of their seats in parliament, and the following government was centre-right wing, based on the Centre Party and Conservatives.) He managed to get the main economic interest groups to sign the new settlement in October 1991, called the Sorsa Accord. By mid-November, none of the individual trade unions or employers' associations had agreed to the settlement, however, and it was obvious that it would fall.[1] After the failure to reach an agreement on the Sorsa Accord, the labour market parties nonetheless managed to agree on a new broad-based settlement 29.11.1991. The settlement was in force

---

[1] Aho 1998, 158.

1992-93, delivering zero wage increases. Although the parties on the labour market managed to reach an agreement, the chairman of SAK was highly critical towards the Centre-led government in its attempts to reduce labour market costs.

> ...the government's role in the negotiations has been beneath contempt and completely different from the previous [government]. The government's representatives have openly supported the views of the employers – even more than the employers themselves.[1]

According to the prime minister of the government, the Finnish labour market organisations were still not prepared for any changes. He noted that one argument expressed by a trade union representative, who opposed the Sorsa Accord in favour of a devaluation of the currency, was that the trade union representatives were not elected to reduce wages, but to increase them. This showed, according to the prime minister, the immaturity of the organisations in reducing labour market costs.[2]

The problematic relationship between the trade union movement and the government continued during its whole period in office. The government came close to a new conflict in 1993, when the central confederation of trade unions made a threat of general strike as a reaction against the government's social, economic and labour market policies.[3] The government had to retreat on its intended labour market policies, including proposed legislative revision on working hours, and make concessions to the trade unions. The issue of working hours legislation therefore became a part of the whole labour market policy in 1993 when the government decided not to submit the bill to the parliament (among the other measures), in order to avoid a general strike. As a result, an already prepared government bill was withdrawn, and the revision of the new working hours law was laid aside during the rest of the non-socialist government's term in office, which ended in 1995.

The problematic relationship between the government and trade union movement also had an effect on the conclusion of a broad-based incomes policy settlement for 1994-95. The conclusion of the settlement failed, when the central confederations of trade unions did not manage to get all their trade union members behind a settlement. The largest trade unions in

---

[1] Incomes policy settlement 29.11.1991. Foreword by Lauri Ihalainen, chairman of SAK.

[2] Aho 1998, 160.

[3] Kauppinen 1994, 333-334.

the manufacturing industry sought after greater pay-rises than a broad-based incomes policy settlement would have provided.[1]

The government therefore had to rely on the individual trade unions and employers' associations, and how they managed to agree on a restrictive policy in their sectoral collective agreements for 1994-95. The round of negotiations on new sectoral collective agreements was opened in November 1993, and by the end of the year, most wage earners were included in sectoral collective agreements. The conclusion of collective agreements at the branch level was much in line with the employers' preferences. After the mid 1980s, employers had made persistent efforts to bring the negotiations on working hours to the firm level, and many of the sectoral collective agreements now included extensive opportunities for making such diverging agreements on working hours.

In the collective agreement for the metal industry, for example, it was stated that the starting point was firm level and individual agreements, and if no such agreements were made, then the collective agreements were to be implemented.[2] One interesting detail from the metal industry's collective agreement on working hours, was the section on how to proceed when making agreements at firm level. It was copied from the proposal for the new working hours act made by the committee. Of a total of six sentences, four were copied in detail, the rest were basically the same.[3] In many of the other collective agreements from autumn 1993, firm level agreements were mentioned. For example, transport, chemistry, glass and book manufacturers all had statements similar to those in the working hours committee text. Working hours, however, were only part of the collective agreements as a whole, but nonetheless a significant part.[4] The only major sector where the opportunity for individual agreements at the firm level was restricted was the paper industry where it was stated in detail which regulations on working hours were to be implemented. In this sector, therefore, there were no opportunities for firm level, individual and other divergent agreements.[5] This meant that the same regulations applied for the whole sector. It is also worth mentioning that the government played a minor role in the conclusion of these collective agreements. The main reason for this was the weak state of the economy, which had been severely

---

[1] Kauppinen 1994, 335.

[2] Collective agreements for the metal industry 1994, 53-54.

[3] Committee proposal 1993: 2, 141; Collective agreement for the metal industry 1994, 94.

[4] Rusanen 1994, 14; Committee proposal 1993: 2, 140-141.

[5] Collective agreement for the paper industry 1994, 16-41.

damaged by the recession. The government had therefore no opportunities to contribute with any improvements in taxation and social benefits, which had been the case during more prosperous years.[1] Another important feature of these sectoral collective agreements were that statements in the committee's proposal for new legislation was included into collective agreements. After 1944, the opposite had often been the case, since what had been agreed in negotiations on collective agreements was later included into legislation.

It may then be asked why there was such a strong resistance from the central confederations trade unions against legislative proposals that were later copied into some collective agreements. One reason behind this is that the statements in the collective agreements would have been unnecessary if they had already been included in legislation. The central confederations of trade unions would have lost some of their influence, manifested through collective agreements. They, therefore, regarded collective agreements as a more important policy making instrument than legislation. The employers could not influence the issue at the main economic interest group level, but nonetheless could influence the issue at the branch level. As a result of the government and trade union strategy, all the negotiating parties were basically satisfied. The employers' associations were satisfied because opportunities for agreements at firm levels were taken into account in many of the major sectoral collective agreements. The central confederations of trade unions were satisfied because the institutionalised decision making context remained unchanged with collective agreements holding their position as an important negotiation arena. And finally, the government was satisfied because peace on the labour market was achieved for two years to come, as a result of the conclusion of sectoral collective agreements. It was therefore an obvious example of a positive sum outcome.

The revision of the working hours legislation did not stop there, however. In a memorandum by a Working Group for Employment, appointed by the Finnish President, the development of a new working hours act was seen as an important instrument in the fight against unemployment. The new government in 1995, led by a Social Democratic prime minister, also stated the importance of a new working hours act for the improvement of employment. A government bill on working hours was planned for submission to the parliament sometime during the spring of 1996. A ministerial working group was consequently set up by the

[1] Kauppinen 1994, 335, 337.

government in 1985, with the task of further developing the working hours legislation. Its objective was to include, in one way or another, some of the new regulations agreed on in sectoral collective agreements for 1994-95 in the development of a new working hours legislation. The stress on opportunities for agreements at firm levels and a reduction of the maximum amount of overtime were seen as the most important objectives.[1] The working group consisted of the independent expert who had functioned as chairperson in the previous committee, a civil servant as the secretary, three representatives from the central confederations of trade unions, and three representatives from the central confederations of employers' associations. The tripartite form of legislative preparation was thus continued. The working group started its work in autumn 1995, and had to finish it by January 31, 1996. It submitted a proposal to the government on February 19, 1996.

The Working Group

The starting point for the group was the conflictual proposal made by the working hours committee in 1993. The issues that had to be resolved were the range of application of the new working hours act, regular working hours by agreements at firm levels, maximum amount of, and payment for overtime, night work and daily rest in connection to EU directives, weekly rest, Sunday work, and the mandatory status of the legislation. An additional task for the working group was to implement the EU working time directive by November 23, 1996 and make the necessary amendments to the Finnish working hours law.

The Range of Application of the Working Hours Act

This section was in itself not particularly difficult to resolve in the group. In the first alternative for a new paragraph by the chairperson (which was identical to the proposal by the working hours committee), the main problems that had to be resolved were the position of workers in supervisory positions, work done in forests, vehicle drivers and workers in the army. The chairperson, supported by the expert on labour legislation, proposed that persons in a supervisory position and all forest work should

---

[1] Tiitinen et al. 1996, 13.

be exempted from the act, and that no special statements for vehicle drivers were to be included. The employers' representatives supported all the proposals made by the chairperson. The workers' representatives strongly objected that the vehicle drivers were to be exempted from the law. Instead, they demanded a separate legislative statement to be implemented on vehicle drivers.[1]

A new sentence was added to the proposal February 7, 1996 when vehicle drivers were included into the act. This was a result of negotiations between the government and the workers' representatives. According to the chairperson '... the vehicle drivers were for some unknown reason included at a very late stage'.[2] The government's involvement in the work became even more obvious in the next section, which dealt with the definition and standard amount of working hours.

The Definition and Regular Amount of Working Hours

The most problematic issues in the working group were what was to be regarded as a standard number of working hours; the role of collective agreements versus legislation, and opportunities for making agreements at the firm level. The parties agreed that the daily working hours were to be set at eight, and weekly working hours at 40. In addition, the chairperson suggested a maximum of nine hours daily if the weekly amount did not exceed 40 hours, while the employers suggested nine hours daily if the total amount did not exceed the maximum annual amount of working hours.[3] The first problematic issue became whether to approve a statement on nine hour working days on condition that the working hours were by the same amount shorter during the next week. In connection with this, there was also a suggestion about abolishing Saturday as the primary day off (besides Sunday) and thereby enable more flexible agreements. If this suggestion had been approved, a general agreement between the parties from 1965, where Saturday was regarded as the second day off, would have become outdated. These issues were not included in the final act.

In the next paragraph, the chairperson suggested that work could be organised according to a maximum of 120 hours over a three-week period, or 80 hours over a two-week period for certain areas. These areas were for example, the police, customs, hospitals, home work and restaurants. This

[1] Memorandum 22.1.1996.

[2] Interview with expert on labour legislation November 6, 1997.

[3] Memorandum January 22, 1996.

section was written at the end according to the proposal by the chairperson. The employers' representatives supported by the chairperson and expert made a proposal about opportunities for making agreements at firm levels on this issue. The workers' representatives did not accept this supplement and it was not included into the final proposal.[1]

In this chapter, opportunities for making collective agreements on working hours as a supplement to legislation were heavily discussed. The reason for including this possibility was to enable divergent working hours agreements, which could take into account the special circumstances in different branches. The right to make these agreements was given to the national trade unions and employers' associations. These organisations could also delegate the power to make the agreements to the firm level, and thereby making it possible to take circumstances at the branch level into account to a higher extent. It was, however, clearly stated that these kinds of agreements were illegal, if they took away advantages that had been granted to employees as statutory rights. Employers who were part of collective agreements also had to give the same benefits to the unorganised employees as to the organised ones.

The next paragraph became the most difficult for the working group, as it had been for the committee, i.e. opportunities for making agreements at the firm level according to legislative regulations, instead of according to collective agreements. The preferences of the different parties had not changed after the previous committee finished its work. The workers' representatives did not approve of opportunities for making firm level agreements as an alternative to national collective agreements, while the employers' representatives were heavily in favour of such opportunities and wanted to remove the mandatory sectoral level from the act. In a summary by the chairperson one week before the committee's deadline, he mentions that this issue was still to a large extent unresolved, especially when it came to the unorganised employers. The preferences expressed by the different parties were completely incompatible.[2] The issue was nonetheless resolved after a meeting between the government and the workers' representative (SAK). After this meeting, the government made a statement on how to proceed with this issue. This statement was almost completely in line with the workers' preferences. According to the chairperson in the previous committee, who functioned as an expert in the subsequent working group, the issues of flexibility and agreements at the

[1] Memorandum January 22, 1996.
[2] Memorandum January 22, 1996.

firm level were at the end diluted. The intentions before the process, where opportunities for more flexibility would be increased, were at the end much less significant than intended. The only area where firm level agreements became possible according to legislation, was the unorganised sector, with employers not bound by any collective agreement. Such employers and employees could, according to legislation, make agreements on the prolonging of daily working hours by a maximum of one hour. The maximum weekly working hours could nonetheless be no more than 45 hours, and had to be no more than a monthly average of 40 hours. This sector, however, is only about 5 per cent of the total labour market. This meant that opportunities for firm level agreements were only possible under the auspices of central confederations of trade unions and employers' associations for 95 per cent of the labour market. The workers' representatives gained an almost complete victory on this issue.[1]

This interpretation was also supported by the chairperson. According to him '...a government representative attended a meeting at 9pm with the 'wishes' of the government that had to be taken into account. They left us no alternative'.[2] According to one of the employers' representatives, the SAK representatives in the committee spent one whole day at the Ministry of Labour, discussing with the government on how to resolve the issue. The result of this discussion was that the workers' representatives gained a complete *torjuntavoitto* ('unexpected victory').[3] The employers' representatives were, naturally, not pleased with the procedure. They had no option, but to accept the procedure.[4] It was, after all, the government's bill they prepared. According to MP Kemppainen (Centre Party), the only reason why the Conservatives, who were in government with the Social Democrats, could accept the final bill was because the upper civil servants were included into the bill.[5] Another reason was the statement where the unorganised employers and their workers could agree on the one-hour flexibility. The decisive role of the government's intervention was also clearly visible in the questions of maximum amount of overtime, and payments for overtime and Sunday work.

---

[1] Interview with expert on labour legislation November 6, 1997.

[2] Interview with civil servant at the Ministry of Labour November 7, 1997.

[3] Interview with expert on labour legislation November 6, 1997. 'Torjuntavoitto' is an often used Finnish word, meaning a victory is achieved against all odds.

[4] Interview with employers' representative 10.11.1997.

[5] Parliamentary protocol 2.5.1996, 1318.

The Maximum Amount of Overtime and Payment for Overtime and Sunday Work

The aim of the chairperson, (and expert), was that the previously implemented supplementary overtime, which had been added to ordinary overtime, was to be withdrawn. They also suggested that the upper limit be set at 138 hours over a four-month period. This proposal was supported by all the other parties in the working group. In addition, the employers' representatives proposed that the maximum annual amount of overtime be set at 416 hours, in line with the EU-directive. The workers' representatives suggested the maximum annual amount of overtime be 200 hours. If the extra overtime was preserved in the new law, it had, according to the workers' representatives, to be no more than 100 hours annually.[1] The basic positions of the parties were that the employers' representatives thought that the maximum amount of allowed overtime should be higher, since the total amount of working hours had been reduced during the last decades. The workers' representatives thought that the maximum amount of allowed overtime was higher in Finland than in other countries, and could therefore be reduced. The parties reached no agreement on this issue.[2]

This issue was again resolved by government intervention. As mentioned earlier, the government and workers' representatives held a meeting outside the group. As a result of this meeting, the government made its own proposal according to which this chapter was to be resolved. They decided that the maximum amount of overtime could be 138 hours over a four-month period, while the annual maximum amount of overtime could be 250 hours. In addition, 80 hours per year of overtime could be agreed upon at the firm level.[3] The government thus made something of a compromise, since 80 hours of overtime could be agreed upon at firm level, a statement which the workers' representatives objected to, but the employer's representatives could approve. When it came to payments for overtime, the employers' representatives were of the opinion that the income from overtime work was higher in Finland than elsewhere and therefore the payments for overtime could be lower. The workers' representatives thought that since the amount of overtime was higher in Finland, then the amount of payments should be relatively higher. Both

---

[1] Memorandum January 22, 1996.

[2] Committee proposal 1993: 2, 143.

[3] Government memorandum February 12, 1996.

parties defended their argument by the same international comparison, but came to completely different conclusions.[1]

The chairperson suggested that the current calculations of percentages were to be preserved. The workers' representatives supported this proposal, while the employers' representatives thought that the amount of extra payment should be reduced. The final proposal was in line with the chairperson and workers' representatives.[2]

Other Issues

Night work In this section, there were proposals about what the limits for night work should be. The chairperson suggested that more than three hours of work done between 10pm and 7am be defined as nightwork. This was also supported by the employers' representatives. The workers' representatives, however, wanted the present limits to be preserved, which was that more than two hours work done between 10pm and 7am was to be defined as night work. The result of this issue was something of a compromise. The three-hour limit was withdrawn and the definition of nightwork became work done between 11pm and 7am.[3]

There was also a suggestion by the chairperson about opportunities for making firm level agreements on this issue, supported by the employers' representatives, but not supported by the workers' representatives. This statement was not included in the proposal by the working group.

Daily rest and Sunday work There were no major discussions on the issues of daily rest and Sunday work. The chairperson proposed statements in line with the EU-directive, the employers' representatives thought that limits stated in the EU-directive were to be applied, while the workers' representatives had only some demands on details. This issue was thus largely solved as a compromise.[4] The result was, that if workers did more than six hours work daily, they were obliged to take at least one hour of rest when they had to have the opportunity to leave the work place. The employer and workers could agree on shorter breaks, but this could be no less than half an hour. If the working day exceeded ten hours, after having done eight hours of work, including breaks, workers had a right to an

[1] Committee proposal 1993: 2, 144.

[2] Memorandum January 22, 1996.

[3] Memorandum January 22, 1996.

[4] Memorandum January 22, 1996.

additional half-hour break after the eight hours. After finishing work, the workers had a right to at least 11 hours of rest. If deemed necessary, exemptions could be made. Vehicle drivers had the right to a minimum of ten hours of rest daily.

Work could be done on Sundays only: a) if it was of the nature that it had to be done on Sundays, b) if it was stated in the working agreement between the employer and employee, and c) if the employee gave his approval for it. The payment for Sunday work was to be raised by 100 per cent from the ordinary payment on weekdays.

The working group made no changes to the committee's proposal. The issues of working hour documents, special statements and entry of force were not discussed, and consequently approved according to the chairperson's proposal.

The EU Working Time Directive

The European Union directive on the organisation of working hours was signed November 13, 1993 and was addressed to all member states of the EU. It was to be implemented no later than November 23, 1996.[1] The purpose of the directive was to improve the living and working conditions of workers in the European Community.[2] This was done by improving conditions in terms of duration and organisation of working hours, and also by providing a diversity of contract forms from open-ended contracts to more fixed-term contracts. Finland became a member of the EU in 1995, and implemented the directive as the new working hours act that entered into force on November 23, 1996. The main difference between the directive and the Finnish working hours act was that the directive did not limit regular daily working hours or working weeks. It did on the other hand, state that the average working hours could not exceed 48 hours per week, but this could be exempted from by means of laws, regulations or collective agreements, on condition that workers were afforded equivalent periods of compensatory rest.[3] Furthermore, the directive did not limit night and shift work and there were no statements about payments for overtime. The structural difference between the directive and Finnish legislation was, therefore, that the Finnish law stated how many working hours were

---

[1] Official Journal of the European Communities 13.12.1993, 307/24.

[2] Official Journal of the European Communities 1993, 18.

[3] Official Journal of the European Communities 1993, 22.

allowed, while the directive stated the mandatory amount of rest.[1] In making the new working hours act, the starting point was fully to implement the directive and thereby prevent disputes over interpretation of the Finnish legislation and its relation to the directive.[2]

The directive applied mainly to a minimum period of daily rest of 11 hours over a 24-hour period and a weekly minimum rest of 24 hours. The directive also applied to certain aspects of night and shiftwork, where for example the average length of night work did not exceed eight hours.[3] The most interesting part of the directive was nonetheless statements about derogations from the directive. It was stated that

> Derogations may be adopted by means of laws, regulations or administrative provisions or by means of collective agreements or agreements between the two sides of industry provided that the workers concerned are afforded equivalent periods of compensatory rest.[4]

This meant that the directive did not prevent the trade unions and employers associations from making their own collective agreements in the future, on condition that they did not take away any advantages that the directive gave. The directive was consequently incorporated into the Finnish working hours law without any major problems in the working group. This was mainly because it did not infringe any Finnish institutional arrangements; it was still possible to derogate from the directive by collective agreements between the national trade unions and employers associations.

Summary and Conclusions

The working group submitted a proposal to the government in March 1996. The government in turn submitted its bill, which was identical to the proposal by the working group, to the parliament. The basic conflict between the workers' and employers' representatives, i.e. the development of opportunities to agree upon working hours increasingly at the firm level, remained unresolved. The government and workers' representatives

[1] Interview with trade union representative November 11, 1997.

[2] Tiitinen et al. 1996, 24.

[3] Official Journal of the European Communities 1993, 19-20.

[4] Official Journal of the European Communities 1993, 22.

decided the final course of events, which left the employers' representatives marginalised, although the statement on 80 hours overtime to be concluded at firm level was in line with their preferences. The employers nonetheless gained at the collective agreements level, since opportunities for making agreements at firm levels had become possible in many of the sectoral collective agreements.

The first question to be answered from this case is whether corporate pluralist arrangements are consensual in character. Issues that are characterised by strongly opposed views and preferences cannot logically be consensual in character without either one, or all of the parties taking part, having to make concessions in order to reach some kind of compromise. Self-interest and consensus are therefore, if not exclusive, at least difficult to combine successfully. As shown in this case, it was in the end self-interest and resources that defined the outcome of the issue. The most important issue, i.e. the development of opportunities for making agreements at the firm level, became characterised by incompatible opinions between the workers' and employers' representatives. It was a case of 'power defines rationality'.[1] The participants demanded that certain statements were to be rewritten according to their own respective preferences. The 'rational' arguments expressed by the chairperson had to yield to the power of the workers' and employer's representatives.

The only aspect of this case that was consensual in character, was the decision by the parties to take part in the process. It is therefore far from obvious that corporate pluralist arrangements are to be regarded as a form of consensus building. Although a solution was found in the end, it was merely a form of power politics that decided the final course of events. The employers' representatives were excluded from the final meetings between the workers' representatives and the government and the outcome was in line with the preferences of the workers' representatives.

This case was furthermore highly characterised by prior norms and requirements. The workers' representatives did not 'free' themselves from their basic preference where the traditional procedure of making arrangements according to the sectoral collective agreements was to be preserved, nor did the employers' representatives 'free' themselves from their basic demand for flexibility. Proposals were not rejected because of acceptable reasons, but were to a high extent rejected because of the main economic interest groups' self interest. Reasoned arguments by the chairperson had in many cases to be withdrawn, since they clashed with the

---

[1] Flyvbjerg 1998, 227.

preferences of the organised interests. The process was not equal, in the sense that the employers were excluded in the final stage of the decision making process, when the government and trade union representatives decided how the final issues of conflict were to be resolved. And finally, reasons persuasive to all were sought after, but not found. It is therefore possible to argue that the formulation process in the working group was not conducted according to the principles of good policy making. On the other hand, a final solution was made and further postponements of the revision of the working hours act would hardly have been a better solution. The revision of the employment contracts act, mentioned in the introduction, provides for an example of a process where no final solution has been reached, even leading to threats of a government crisis. The following question is how the issue was handled by the parliament, and what the revision of the working hours act can tell about the relationship between the parliamentary committee for labour affairs and the main economic interest groups.

6 Parliamentary Deliberation – Formal Rules and Informal Practices

The aim of this chapter is to evaluate whether the Finnish parliament is still as subservient to pressure group influence in the 1990s when it comes to labour market policy making as was commonly regarded to be the case after the conclusion of broad based settlements from 1968 onwards. The main focus will be on the parliamentary standing Committee for Labour Affairs, since it deals with all matters related to the labour market. The chapter is divided into three parts. In the first, the formal decision making procedures of the parliament are explained, as well as the formal and informal procedures of the Committee for Labour Affairs. The second part is an evaluation of the parliamentary deliberation of the working hours case. These two parts lead to the third and final part, which is a discussion on whether there has been, or still is, a democratic deficit in Finland when it comes to labour market policy making. The common view among MPs has been that corporate pluralist arrangements reduce the role of the parliament and therefore also lead to a democratic deficit. A contrasting view is that the involvement of organised interests in public policy making does not pose a threat against democratic institutions, but is to be seen as an alternative form of democracy.[1]

The main theoretical problem in the corporatist literature was how to describe the relationship between organised interests and the state. As noted in chapter one, alternative approaches were made, including different subcategorisations of corporatism as a concept. The theoretical relationship between states and organised interests remained underdeveloped in the corporatist literature, however, but empirical findings nonetheless pointed

[1] Jordan and Richardson 1987, 287.

to a highly regulated relationship between them in certain areas. The main economic interest groups had gained access to different boards, commissions and committees, and had been asked opinions in matters of their concerns. In an axiomatic statement from 1966, Rokkan noted that votes count but resources decide.[1] The electoral channel was seen as subservient to the corporate channel.

A decline in the role of parliaments was a common theme in the 1970s. Besides the increasing influence of organised interests at the cost of parliamentary power, two other reasons behind the decline-thesis were often expressed. The decline was seen as a result of large and cohesive parties 'colonising' the parliament, which weakened its legislative functions. In keeping with the official party line, MPs had become members of parties, rather than members of parliament. Another reason for a decline was a considerable growth in the scale and scope of government, which was a result of the increasing tasks the state faced in its work for economic growth and welfare. This had led to a growing need for specialists and government officials, who consequently had increased their influence at the cost of parliamentary power.[2]

Authors started to challenge the parliamentary decline-thesis in the 1980s. Arter's comparative analysis of the Nordic countries in the mid 1980s, concluded that the parliaments in this region did not fit into the common picture of the declining importance in parliaments.

> The Nordic parliaments have had the political power to make their views heard in the deliberation and adoption of government bills and have at times asserted themselves to influence the course of events.[3]

Another comparative analysis from 1992, furthermore concluded, that Nordic parliaments were no rubber-stamp, but had increased in importance in relation to governments. The reason for this was that disagreements over the nature of problems and their possible solutions had become more common in Sweden, Norway and Denmark, and consequently led to a revitalisation of parliaments in these countries. Finland was a possible exception since it was characterised more by consensus than conflict.[4] Other research also suggested that the parliamentary decline thesis was

---

[1] Rokkan 1966, 106.

[2] Arter 1984, 31-35.

[3] Arter 1984, 416.

[4] Damgaard 1992, 203-204.

invalid. In an edited volume of parliaments in seven European countries (Great Britain, France, Italy, Germany, Ireland, the Netherlands and Sweden) the Italian, Dutch and Swedish parliaments were seen as strong policy-influencing bodies.[1] The two Chambers of the Italian parliament could amend government proposals without restriction. This was a result of both weak governments and weak government policy making procedures.[2] In the Netherlands the parliament had been able greatly to increase its activism when it came to amendments of bills. In addition, the consociational character of Dutch politics in the 1960s to 1970s, with an extensive inter-elite consensus, had given away to more competitive procedures, thereby increasing the opportunities for parliamentary intervention in policy making.[3] The Swedish parliament was regarded as a strong policy-influencing body since it had been able to take part in all policy making stages, from formulation to implementation.[4] A bold statement even characterised the 1990s as 'the age of parliaments'.[5]

When it comes to the workhorses in parliaments, the committees, another conclusion from Nordic comparative research in 1984, was that they were regarded as less important as negotiating sites than both the parliamentary party groups, and other arenas outside the parliament. They could not therefore be compared to the important policy-influencing committees of the US House of Representatives, where the members had a strong orientation towards the House, emphasised expertise and identified strongly with the committee. The committees were on the other hand more important than the committees in Westminster where the members lacked a sense of identification with the committee and where expertise was played down.[6] The Nordic parliamentary committees fell somewhere in between these two polarised categories.

In a recent comparative analysis of 16 countries in Western Europe, parliamentary committees have been considered as playing meaningful and important roles in the legislative work. The main reason for this has been that parliaments worldwide have developed their internal structure over a number of decades. This has in particular meant a more central role for the

---

[1] Norton 1990.

[2] Furlong 1990, 62-65.

[3] Gladdish, 1990, 116-117.

[4] Arter 1990, 139.

[5] Copeland and Patterson 1994, 1.

[6] Arter 1984, 207.

parliamentary committees, which are regarded as being among the most significant internal organisational features of modern parliaments.[1]

Finland is no exception in this sense. Before the constitutional amendments in 1992, when the antiquated rules of majority voting were abolished, a revision in 1990 had 'institutionalised' the parliamentary committees. Before the revision, there were five permanent and eight temporary committees in parliament. After the revision, there was to be a Grand Committee and an additional number of permanent special committees. If necessary, temporary committees could be appointed to a special task. The Finnish parliament currently consists of the Grand Committee and 14 permanent committees, in comparison to the five permanent and eight temporary ad hoc committees before.

The current trend in parliamentary research is underlining the importance of parliaments and their committees. In order to find out whether the Finnish parliament constitutes an important arena in Finnish labour market policy making, semistructured interviews were conducted in 1998, with one member from each political party represented in the Committee for Labour Affairs.[2] The focus of the interviews was mainly, on which rules and practices applied to contemporary labour market policy making in Finland. The questions asked the MPs covered such aspects of parliamentary decision making, as how work in the committee was organised, what the relationships to other actors inside and outside parliament were and the members' perceptions of their role in overall labour market policy making. The analysis therefore focused on the relationship between the preferences of the MPs, and the formal rules and informal practices they confirmed to.

Formal rules are found in constitutional codes that define the principal duties and responsibilities of an organisation. These rules set the framework for how the parliament works. Such formal rules can never be fully specified, however, and informal practices therefore become more influential. These practices also become more interesting because their informal character may reveal aspects of decision making that cannot be detected by a mere focus on formal codes for decision making.

---

[1] Strøm 1997, 55.

[2] Members in the 1995-1999 parliamentary period were: SDP: Reijo Lindroos (chairperson), Tuula Haatainen, Pirkko Peltomo, Heikki Rinne, Marja-Leena Viljamaa. KOK: Kari Kantalainen, Anne Knaapi, Heikki Koskinen, Outi Siimes. KESK: Kyösti Karjula, Hannu Kemppainen, Armas Komi (substitute chairperson), Maija-Liisa Veteläinen. RKP: Raimo Tiilikainen. VAS: Anne Huotari, Jorma Vokkolainen. EVIR: Pertti Virtanen.

The informal practices are consequently more difficult to pin down than the formal rules, but at least five separate variants can be differentiated. The first two are renomination and re-election. The third informal practice MPs have to take into account is their own ambition to advance within the party hierarchy, and the fourth is their aspirations for higher positions within the parliament (for example to become the speaker of parliament or chairman of a committee).[1] Fifthly, they also have to take into account extra-parliamentary constraints posed by organised interests. The MPs are, of course, not formally obliged to obey any pressure from organised interests, but this does not mean that they do not have to comply with them informally.

Parliamentary Decision Making

The most important way in which matters are brought forward for the parliament to decide on is by bills, either submitted by the government or by individual MPs. These are submitted to the speaker of the parliament, who, after discussion with the Speaker's Council, decides on when, or if, the matter is to be handled by the parliament. The Speaker's Council consists of the parliamentary speaker, deputy speakers and the chairmen of the parliamentary committees. Bills by individual MPs can be either in the form of proposals for legislative amendments *(lakialoite)*, budgetary proposals *(raha-asia aloite)* or so-called petitionary motions *(toivomusaloite),* with a request that the parliament urges the government to take action on a specific matter. Individual MPs may also submit written questions to the Speaker's Council. It is then up to the council to decide whether the question is to be handled by the parliament or not. The Speaker's Council may also decide whether to allow oral question times, where the MPs have a right to pose short oral questions to ministers of the government. MPs may also submit questions on important administrative or foreign matters for the government to answer. These kinds of questions must be submitted in writing to the Speaker's Council, signed by at least four MPs. The minister of government, to whom the written question has been addressed, must reply within three weeks. There is no debate on these questions. In 1998, 286 government bills, 1744 written questions and 296 oral questions were submitted to parliament.

---

[1] Strøm 1997, 167-170.

After a bill has been submitted to parliament, it is usually discussed in a preliminary debate in plenary session. After this debate, it is submitted to a standing committee for detailed considerations. The committee writes a report on the bill, after which it is debated in plenum as first reading. This reading is a general debate on the proposed bill and no decisions are made at this stage. After the first reading the bill comes up to a second reading where it is debated in detail. If necessary, each section may be voted on. After the second reading, the bill comes up to the third and final reading, where the bill as a whole is either approved or rejected. Amendments are at this stage no longer possible. All bills of non-constitutional character are approved by a simple majority. If the bill is approved by the parliament, it is sent to the president of the republic for ratification. If the president refuses to ratify the parliament's proposal, it is returned to the next session of parliament. If the parliament also approves the bill this time, it comes into force without the president's ratification. Up to the 1960s the president refused to ratify a bill on approximately 50 occasions, mainly due to technical deficiencies in the proposed bills. In the 1970s, the long-serving president Urho Kekkonen used the threat of non-ratification veto as a form of political weapon. This, however, happened only on some occasions.[1] The threat of non-ratification veto has not been used by the last two presidents of the republic (Mauno Koivisto 1982-1994 and Martti Ahtisaari 1994-2000).

The state budget is dealt with in a slightly different manner. It is submitted in early September and introduced to the parliament by a speech by the minister of finance. At the end of a preliminary debate in parliament, the Finance Committee completes a report on the budget, which is to be submitted in early December. The budget is then approved by parliament in a single reading, normally including hundreds of votes. Furthermore, amendments of constitutional laws are possible in two different ways. In the first, the bill is approved by a simple majority, after which it is left in abeyance until after the next parliamentary election. If the newly elected parliament approves the amendment, (this time with a two-thirds majority), it becomes law. The second procedure is to declare the amendment urgent with a five-sixth majority, after which it can be approved during the same parliamentary session by a two-thirds majority.[2]

---

[1] Arter 1984, 292.

[2] The constitutional acts in Finland are: the Form of government Act, the parliament Act, the Act on the Right of parliament to Examine the Legality of Official Actions by Members of the Council of State and the Chancellor of Justice, and the High Court of Impeachment Act.

A new constitution act enters into force on March 1, 2000, which increases the role of the parliament at the cost of the president's powers. The president maintains a right to dissolve the parliament and order new elections. This, however, can only be made on the proposal by the prime minister, provided that the different parliamentary groups and the speaker of parliament have been consulted. The situation before the 1990s was that the president could without formalised consultation dissolve the parliament and order new elections. All parliament acts still have to be ratified by the president. If he or she refuses, the handling of the law returns to parliament but if the parliament again approves the bill, it comes into force without the president's approval. If the president refused to ratify an act before the 1990s it could not be handled by the parliament again until after the next parliamentary election. Although foreign policy is still the president's main duty, Finland's relationship to the EU as a member state has led to an increasing role for the parliament. The parliament's views in EU matters are normally expressed by the Grand Committee, except in matters dealing with EU foreign and security policy when the parliament views are expressed by the Foreign Affairs Committee. Foreign policy in Finland in the 1990s has thus become more dualistic with the president still conducting the main lines of foreign policy whilst EU affairs are largely in the hands of the government and parliament. The position of the parliament has consequently been strengthened vis-à-vis the president by the new constitution.

Formal Rules for the Parliamentary Committees

The main parliamentary work is done in the standing committees, which have often been labelled the workhorses of parliament. The committees' work is formally regulated in the Procedure of parliament Act. Besides the Grand Committee, the permanent committees are: Foreign Affairs Committee, Committee for Constitutional Law, Legal Affairs Committee, Finance Committee, Administration Committee, Transport and Communications Committee, Committee for Agriculture and Forestry, Defence Committee, Committee for Education and Culture, Social Affairs and Health Committee, Economic Affairs Committee, Committee for Labour Affairs, the Environment Committee and the Committee for the Future. The Grand Committee has 25 full members and 13 substitute members. In addition, the MP representing the Åland islands is entitled to participate in its meetings. The Finance Committee has 21 members and 19 substitute members, while the other committees have 17 members and 9 substitute members respectively. (Temporary committees must have a minimum of 11 members.)

Table 6.1 Workload in terms of legal reports on government bills and other expressed official opinions of the committees 1991-96

	1991	1992	1993	1994	1995	1996
Grand Committee	1	8	8	12	5	7
Foreign Affairs Committee	10	29	26	25	28	51
Committee for Constitutional Law	20	49	54	54	28	54
Legal Affairs Committee	10	21	29	38	19	42
Finance Committee	74	100	86	110	60	81
Administration Committee	17	23	34	39	22	34
Transport and Communications Committee	6	15	14	33	16	26
Committee for Agriculture and Forestry	26	39	38	53	25	52
Defence Committee	6	9	6	9	6	5
Committee for Education and Culture	14	26	33	41	18	28
Social Affairs and Health Committee	32	67	68	66	33	57
Economic Affairs Committee	26	61	50	76	42	48
Committee for Labour Affairs	12	18	17	21	11	34
Environment Committee	13	23	17	41	16	15
Committee for the Future	-	-	-	1	-	-
Total	267	488	480	619	329	534

Source: Parliamentary Protocols

The Finance Committee has the largest workload when it comes to the handling of government bills. This is quite obvious by reference to its task: the handling of the annual state budget and all the annual taxation laws. The Defence and Future Committees, together with the Grand Committee, have made the least reports and opinions. This is not to say that these committees have a lighter workload - the Grand Committee after all deals with all EU matters. Its task is to ensure that the parliament can exert influence over matters dealt with in the EU. It also expresses the views of the parliament regarding EU proposals. These views are to be regarded as politically binding on the government. It may also request information from the EU on matters that are under preparation. Before an amendment of the Parliament Act in 1992, every bill, except the annual state budget, had to be sent to the Grand Committee after the first reading in parliament. After the amendment, the Grand Committee participates in the scrutinisation of bills, only if parliament so decides in the first reading. However, if amendments are made to bills in the second reading in plenary sessions, they are automatically submitted to the Grand Committee for scrutinisation.[1]

Table 6.1 is highly indicative, and there is no clear tendency over the 1990s to indicate whether workload is increasing, or decreasing, when it comes to bills and other motions. One aspect of parliamentary work that without doubt has increased during the 1990s, is the flow of information. This has not been reflected in the official workload in the committees, however, since '... 95 per cent of received mail usually goes directly in the bin'.[2] The introduction of part time personal assistants for MPs in the 1990s has nonetheless improved the situation when it comes to dealing with the flow of information.

The parliament decides on the Speaker's Council's proposal as to which committee a matter is to be submitted. A committee may also, on its

---

[1] The rest of the Committees deal with matters that fall under their respective names. The Foreign Affairs Committee deals with matters connected to relationships with other countries, including the foreign and security policy of the EU. In these matters, the Committee has the same rights to receive information and express the view of the parliament, as the Grand Committee. The Committee for Constitutional Law deals with all constitutional acts, the electoral legislation and the state administration at the highest ministerial level. It also deals with legislative matters connected to the autonomy of the Åland Islands, as well as matters connected to citizenship, language, and political party legislation. The Legal Affairs Committee deals with the general laws, like family, criminal and civil laws, as well as legislation of the courts. The Finance Committee is the only committee with subcommittees, since its main task is to make proposals for the annual state budget. Its nine subcommittees deal with matters on administration, defence and security, taxation, education and research, agriculture, traffic, trade and industry, social and labour affairs, and the environment. The Administration Committee deals with the organisation of state administration that is not dealt with by the Committee for Constitutional Law. Its main objective is local administration, regional policy and state personnel policy. The Transport and communications Committee deals with air, railway and sea regulations, as well as radio and TV communications, while the Committee for Agriculture and Forestry deals with agriculture and forest issues. The Committee for the Future is appointed with the task of evaluating the government's programme for the future. It evaluates technological knowledge and success in other countries, identifying to what extent they are applicable to Finland. It also investigates how to improve the working procedures and relationship between the government and parliament.

[2] Interview with MP, 15.5.1998.

own initiative, demand information or explanations from ministries on issues that the committee is responsible for. In general, the committee should deal with matters in the following order:[1]

1. Statements to be issued on the basis of a report by the government.
2. Decisions on the state budget made by parliament but not ratified by the president of the republic.
3. Legislative proposals left in abeyance and unratified acts.
4. Government proposals.
5. Statements to the Grand Committee or Foreign Affairs Committee on EU matters.
6. Legislative proposals which have been signed by no fewer than 100 MPs.
7. Other reports.
8. Statements to other committees regarding private member's bills.
9. Bills.
10. Petitionary motions.

The highest priority is given to the annual reports the government is required to submit to parliament. These reports are sent to a special committee for consideration, and subsequently handled by the parliament in a single reading. The government may also submit reports regarding the state administration, or relations with foreign states. These reports are discussed in plenary session, but do not have to go through the committee stage if it is deemed unnecessary. Before 1983, government bills came on top of the list, with private members initiatives at the bottom. After 1983, both government and individual bills are given the lowest priority. Points number five and six above were added in 1994.

There are two readings on each matter in a committee. In the first reading, the committee makes a preliminary decision on the content, and in the second, it makes the final decision based on a draft by the committee's secretary. Each member in the committee must be given an opportunity to express his or her view on the matter. Each member may also ask outside experts to express their views on the matter in the first reading. Dissenting opinions may be submitted in written form to be added at the end of the committee's report.

Committees meet one to four times a week depending on their workload and all meetings are secret. Members of the committees are

[1] Procedure of Parliament, section 18b.

appointed at the first plenary session a new parliament convenes. The composition of the committees is normally the same throughout the parliamentary term. Temporary committees may be appointed at any time during the parliamentary term, and are normally appointed until their task has been completed. The chairperson of the committee is chosen at its first meeting. The composition of committees follows as exactly as possible the proportion of MPs between parties in the parliament as a whole.

The committee's work is therefore regulated in a fairly detailed manner. The work of individual members of committees is also formally regulated, but in an extremely general manner. In the parliament Act it is stated that:

> A Member of Parliament has a duty to uphold justice and truth in his or her action. The member is therefore responsible to uphold the constitution, but is bound by no other regulations.[1]

The important object of analysis therefore becomes what additional informal rules or practices apply to committees and their work. While the formal decision making rules for a committee as a whole cannot be overlooked, rules for individual MPs can be developed in a free manner, on condition that they uphold justice and truth.[2] The objective of the rest of this section is to focus on the informal rules in the Committee for Labour Affairs.

Informal Rules for the Committee for Labour Affairs

The informal rules can be related to how members are assigned to committees, how decisions are made, what external pressure the MPs have to take into account and how the political ambition of individual MPs affects their work. Since all the interviews were conducted with members of the 1995-99 parliamentary session, the tables are also based on MP data from the same period. A brief note on the reliability of this section is necessary. The results are based on six interviews only, each MP interviewed representing a different party. The results can therefore not be seen as representative for the parliament as a whole and they remain

---

[1] Parliament Act, section 11.

[2] On only four occasions since 1917 has an MP been charged with offences against the constitution. The last time this happened was in 1993, when the Minister of Trade and Industry K.Juhantalo, was convicted for connecting his personal financial affairs with his work as a Minister of the government.

indicative without more extensive and thorough studies of Finnish MPs.[1] The results can nonetheless be regarded as fairly representative of how the Committee for Labour Affairs works and the opportunities and constraints that its members have to take into account. These views are supported by tables that include data of all MPs as well as previous research.

Committee assignments The principle behind committee assignments is based on parliamentary age and the position within the party hierarchy. This is fairly evident from the following table. The first column is the percentage of members in the committees that were elected in the 1995 election, the second column is the proportion that were elected in the 1991 election, the third column elected in the 1987 election, the fourth in the 1983 election, the fifth in the 1979 election and the sixth in the 1975 election.[2]

Table 6.2 Number of periods in parliament (percentage)

	1995	1991	1987	1983	1979	1975
Parliament in total	41.5	21.0	16.5	17.0	2.0	2.0
Government	18.8	18.8	31.2	12.5	12.5	6.2
Grand Committee	36.0	24.0	20.0	20.0	-	-
Foreign Affairs Committee	5.9	17.6	23.5	41.2	5.9	5.9
Committee for Constitutional Law	52.9	29.4	5.9	11.8	-	-
Legal Affairs Committee	58.8	5.9	29.4	5.9	-	-
Finance Committee	-	33.2	28.6	28.6	4.8	4.8
Administration Committee	58.9	17.6	17.6	5.9	-	-
Transport and Communications Com.	58.8	11.8	23.5	-	5.9	-
Com. for Agriculture and Forestry	64.7	17.6	11.8	5.9	-	-
Defence Committee	58.8	23.5	17.7	-	-	-
Committee for Education and Culture	70.6	17.6	11.8	-	-	-
Social Affairs and Health Committee	47.1	29.4	23.5	-	-	-
Economic Affairs Committee	75.0	12.6	6.2	6.2	-	-
Committee for Labour Affairs	70.6	17.6	5.9	5.9	-	-
Environment Committee	64.7	23.5	5.9	5.9	-	-
Committee for the Future	64.7	11.8	5.9	17.6	-	-

[1] For a thorough analysis of Swedish MPs, see Esaiasson and Holmberg 1996.

[2] Data from the MPs was collected from their respective homepages on the Internet (http://www.eduskunta.fi).

The more attractive and important committees comprise longer-serving parliamentarians and MPs in a leading position within their respective party. It is also generally accepted that an expert on foreign policy or public economy, without a front position in the party or any parliamentary experience, will not be elected to the Foreign Affairs or Finance Committee. It is therefore not the knowledge or expertise of individual MPs that count when the most attractive and important committees are appointed, but their position within the party hierarchy. The reasons behind the attractiveness of the Foreign Affairs and Finance Committees may be difficult to pin down. One pragmatic reason for the status of the Foreign Affairs Committee is that it involves more visits abroad than the other. The allocation of travel money to this committee is therefore far higher than any other committees.[1] The Finance Committee has been regarded particularly important as it deals with the annual state budget. A rise in the importance of individual ministries and departments has nonetheless diminished the importance of this committee. In December 1997, some members of parliament complained about their lack of influence in the making of the new annual budget for 1998. They thought that the bureaucrats and economic experts had obtained too much influence, which had reduced the parliamentary role to merely approve of decisions taken elsewhere.[2]

According to Arter (1984), women in the Finnish parliament are more likely to become members of the so-called lightweight committees.[3] This is still also the case. In the 1995 parliament, 34 per cent were women. (After the last parliamentary election in 1999, 37 per cent are women.) They were over-represented in the Grand Committee, Committee for Education and Culture, Social Affairs and Health Committee, Economic Affairs Committee, the Committee for Labour Affairs, and the Environment Committee. The attractiveness of the Grand Committee may change as it was bestowed with all EU-matters in 1995. Since the 1999 parliamentary election, the committee is also chaired by the leader of the largest opposition party.

The members of the Committee for Labour Affairs had the following background. There were two members who worked as workers' representatives in companies, one secretary at a trade union, one farmer, one nurse, one office secretary, four executive officers in the public sector,

[1] Interview with MP, 15.5.1998.

[2] Hufvudstadsbladet 16.12.1997.

[3] Arter 1984, 200.

one executive officer in the private sector, one medical doctor, one lecturer, one student, one army admiral and two psychologists. None of them had any higher position within their respective parties, and 12 of the 17 representatives were on their first period in parliament. Besides the two members who had worked as workers' representatives, and the member who worked for a trade union, it is close to impossible to determine whether the rest were experts on labour market issues. They nonetheless represented different backgrounds, and the committee was in that sense characterised by a common knowledge of the labour market field in general. It is also reasonable to assume that the members of the committee were interested in its work, since appointments to committees usually proceed according to preferences expressed by the MPs, except for the Foreign Affairs and Finance Committees. The exception may be the Conservative Party, where the Committee for Labour Affairs was not considered very attractive.[1] The left wing parties, on the other hand, regarded the committee as more important, with members willing to take part in its work.[2]

Decision making procedures in the Committee for Labour Affairs All those interviewed were of the same opinion in one respect: the parliament as a whole function well in theory, but is extremely inefficient in practice. The reasons for this inefficiency are the working procedures of plenum. All the readings are, more or less, a necessary formality. The MPs do not regard the readings as meaningful, and so absentees are common. Another great problem in parliamentary work is that the preliminary debate (lähetekeskustelu) in plenary sessions is not transmitted live to the committee that has made the preliminary work. The MPs, in other words, do not know as to what has been said in the plenum regarding the matter under discussion, if they have not themselves been present in the debate, or listened to the debate over the internal radio. 'Nothing' is ever changed as a result of discussions in plenum, and same matters are usually debated over and over again, since the issues under discussion cannot provide material for discussions over several days.[3] It may, however, be a slight overstatement to say that nothing is ever changed in plenary sessions. In 1920, only 58 per cent of government bills passed the plenary stage without modification. In 1937 the figure had risen to 78 per cent and in 1964 to 94

[1] Interviews with MPs 13-14.5.1998.

[2] Interview with MP 13.5.1998.

[3] Interviews with MPs 13.5, 20.5.1998.

per cent.[1] In 1983 the figure was 97 per cent. The percentage of bills that was accepted by parliament without any changes, either in committees, or plenary sessions, was 49 per cent in 1929, 45 per cent in 1951, 49 per cent in 1960, 62 per cent in 1972 and 70 per cent in 1983.[2] The absolute majority of parliamentary changes to government bills are therefore made at the committee stage, and plenary sessions are to be seen more as a necessary formality.

In a formal regulation for all the committees, it is stated that decisions are made by voting if the committee is not unanimous. In practice, however, voting takes place extremely seldom in the Committee for Labour Affairs. Instead, it is most often the case, that the members from the opposition parties write minority reports and the members of the parties in government keep to the official party line. The table shows that almost all dissenting opinions to the committee's reports between 1991 and 1996 were expressed by members from the opposition parties.

Table 6.3 Reports to parliament and minority opinions

	1991	1992	1993	1994	1995	1996
Number of reports	9	15	13	11	7	18
Total of minority opinions/minority opinions by opposition parties	5/4	11/8	5/5	5/5	-/-	3/3

Source: Parliamentary Protocols

Issues are furthermore connected to a great extent. The most often used word for this in Finland is equivalent to horse-trade *(lehmäkauppa)* where you give something to the opponent on one question, and receive something else on another issue. It is thus a kind of positive sum bargaining, where parties can compromise on issues they do not regard as important for them, but that are more important for the other parties, and vice versa. Matters belonging to different committees may also be connected and bargained on. This way of dealing with issues is more a rule than an exception in the way the Finnish parliament works.

External constraints The Committee for Labour Affairs works relatively independently from the influence of the various parliamentary party groups.

[1] Nousiainen 1977, 113-131.

[2] Anckar 1992, 182.

Only if difficult and conflictual issues are on the agenda, the leaders of the party groups may, together with the chairperson of the committee, discuss the issue and try to reach an agreement beforehand. This seldom happens, however. The major problem for the Committee for Labour Affairs is that the system, with the main economic interest groups taking part in the preparatory work, leaves little room for change, since all matters are more or less decided beforehand. This does not mean that they are totally isolated from what happens on the labour market. The committee is usually invited to weekly discussions and seminars with the central confederations of trade unions. In addition, the individual MPs, depending on their background, have their own meetings and contacts with the labour market. The committee is furthermore greatly dependent on the Ministry of Labour, which in turn is greatly dependent on its civil servants. According to one MP, in trying to make changes to some proposals some civil servants at the Ministry of Labour have objected this and said that not one thing can be changed, since there is already an agreement on this matter between the parties on the labour market. 'Some lousy civil servant comes and tell us what we can and cannot do'.[1]

According to another representative, however, the biggest surprise was the friendliness of the civil servants and opportunity to have open discussions with them.[2] The individual MPs have opportunities for individual initiatives, even though it is extremely difficult to get their views heard. If successful, this action must be situated at the earliest possible stage of the decision making process, to some extent demanding an instinct for where the centre of power is located.[3]

There are also other examples from this committee on the difficulty to take individual initiatives. After extensive and thorough work, one member managed to get a detail in the explanatory notes of the peacekeeper employment security bill, not the bill itself, however.[4] A further illustration was when some members in the committee developed some points on how to reduce unemployment. After thorough consideration they sent their six-page proposal to the President of the republic (who had earlier appointed a working group with the task of evaluating how to reduce unemployment), and asked for audience on the matter. However, they were never granted

[1] Interview with MP 15.5.1998.

[2] Interview with MP 20.5.1998.

[3] Interviews with MPs 13-14.5.1998.

[4] Lengthy motivations are always added to laws that explain how it is to be interpreted and why the legislative statements are formulated the way they are.

one.[1] According to one member, being in opposition gives more room for individual influence over the majority's policy, since members from government parties are usually more bound to the official government line, and diverging opinions are thus difficult for them to express.

These are, of course, only some details, but nevertheless, they show that the members of the committee face great obstacles in their efforts to take individual initiatives. This also underlines the secondary importance of the remiss system where external experts are heard on subjects. It is merely a formality, since very little is ever changed in the committee when the questions are dealt with elsewhere. One must remember, however, that the Committee for Labour Affairs is most probably an exception when it comes to the external constraints that are posed upon the work of its members. According to one MP all decision making by the committee is extremely difficult. Nothing can be changed without the approval of the extra parliamentary forces. In contrast, the Committee for Social Affairs works in a different manner and the issues dealt with there are discussed more openly, with different opinions taken into account to a much higher extent.[2]

The views of a more normative issue over who should have the power to make labour market policy differed greatly between the MPs. According to representatives of the left-wing parties, the organised interests have a very important position. They play a more important role in transforming the needs of the labour market into political decisions. The non-socialist representatives were of the opposite opinion. They thought that the organised interests have too great an influence over labour market policy making.

Political ambition A common problem the members face, are situations where their individual preferences do not harmonise with the official party line. If they follow their conviction and vote against the party line, they reduce their future chances of gaining higher positions within the party. There are, however, no formal rules for party discipline, merely informal ones. Party discipline is especially important when it comes to the Left-Wing Alliance. After two votes against the official party line, to a large extent decided by the chairperson of the party, one is automatically out of the party group (in theory at least).[3] Another good example is the chairperson from SDP who sometimes has expressed his own opinion

---

[1] Interview with MP 15.5.1998.

[2] Interview with MP 14.5.1998.

[3] Interview with MP 13.5.1998.

instead of the party line. He obviously had gained an important position within the parliament, at the cost of an important position within the party hierarchy.

> ...look at me, I have never gained any position in the party hierarchy. On the other hand, no one walks over me in parliament over issues that belong to the committee.[1]

The only exception here may be the Swedish People's Party, which has a more liberal view on this matter than the other parties, where its members are able to take more individual initiatives. According to its representative in the committee, it is possible to express and work for personal views, even if they do not completely harmonise with the Party's official views. All of the members that were interviewed, nonetheless, regarded the parliamentary work as meaningful and intended to continue their work, if elected. The members regarded it to be the parliament's own fault, if its importance had been on a decline. It was consequently up to the parliament itself to increase its role and importance. It was furthermore obvious, that members striving for more leading positions in their party thought that they were representing the party line, and not any individual interests. By aiming at several periods in parliament, they had larger opportunities of gaining more important positions, both in the party and within the parliamentary institutions.

Summary

So far, this evaluation of the Committee for Labour Affairs does not fit into the assumption of the importance of parliamentary committees. If the members wanted to advance in the party hierarchy, they had to comply with the official party line. Dissenting opinions to the committee's reports were also rare among the members of the parties in government. In this respect it is therefore possible to state that they were members of parties, rather than members of parliament. Although the committee had regularised contacts with the organisations on the labour market, when it came to the practical law making, they had small opportunities for making an impact. All labour legislation had been discussed and prepared in tripartite meetings between the main economic interest groups and experts on legislation. The committee members faced great obstacles if they tried to

---

[1] Interview with MP 13.5.1998.

change something that had already been agreed upon. They also thought that the civil servants of the Ministry of Labour played a decisive role, since they prepared all legislation. All members furthermore agreed that the parliament functioned well in theory, but badly in practice. The plenary sessions were more or less seen as redundant.

All members expressed the same view that the influence of the extra-parliamentary forces was the most decisive for the committee as a whole. This also points to the fact that participation and discussions between the committee and the organised interests did not count for much in practical decision making. Other informal rules that counted on an individual level were whether the MPs intended to seek higher positions within their respective parties. Aspirations for committee assignments were not seen as important as aspirations within the party. The aim of the next section is to evaluate how the working hours case was handled and whether it harmonised with the overall views expressed by the members of the Committee for Labour Affairs.

The Working Hours Case

The government's bill on a new working hours act was submitted to parliament on 22 April 1996. It was discussed for the first time in parliament 2 May 1996 in the preliminary debate. After this debate the Committee for Labour Affairs handled the bill in detail whereafter it was debated at the first reading on June 11. The second reading took place on June 12 and the bill was enacted by parliament at third reading on June 18. The bill was thus dealt with fairly rapidly, since it took less than two months to get it enacted by parliament.

There was a lively submission debate on the issue. It was opened by the minister of labour who presented the main outline of the proposed legislation. She was grateful to the parties on the labour market taking part in the preparation of the law, despite the fact that the government had to step in and resolve the main issues of conflict. She also regarded the revised law as up to then the most modern working hours law in Europe, as well as the most significant legislative development on the labour market for a long time, which enabled the unorganised field of employers and employees to make agreements at the firm level.[1] There were in all 55 speeches by 21 different MPs in the submission debate. The most discussed

[1] Parliamentary Protocol 2.5.1996, 1316.

subjects were the maximum amount of overtime, questions of flexibility and agreements at the firm level, the impact the new law will have on employment and finally, the question of the influence by interest organisations in the preparations of the government bill.

In connection to the government's submission of the new working hours act, two private members' bills had also been submitted. The first bill, signed by 48 MPs, proposed that the regular amount of working hours should be set to a maximum of six hours daily, or 30 hours weekly. Their main argument was that this would be a step forward in attempts to create employment. The second bill, signed by 56 MPs, proposed that a temporary law should be enacted where the statement on maximum amount of overtime in the government bill was to be reduced over the coming five years. Their main argument was that this would have a positive effect on employment. In this debate there were in all 15 speeches by ten different MPs. The speeches were mainly about the impact on employment that these two bills would have. (32 MPs had signed both of the private members' bills.)

The government's bill and the private members bills were subsequently sent to the Committee for Labour Affairs for consideration. The committee asked the opinion of 33 different organisations and experts on the issue. Of these, 15 were workers' organisations, nine employers' associations and nine civil servants and other experts from universities. After hearing these expert opinions, the committee asked a civil servant at the Ministry of Labour to give a summary of all the opinions. According to the civil servant's summary, the opinions expressed by these different organised interests and other experts were of the kind that did not demand any changes in the government's bill, most of the opinions being merely polemical. Some of the opinions were only about a specific area and therefore unable to be solved by a general law. Some of the opinions were critical towards the bill, but since, according to the civil servant, there was an agreement between the central confederations on these issues, they demanded no revision. The only opinion taken into account was a statement made by an expert from a university on the question of punishment for breaches of the law. This was, however only a question of legal formality.[1] The committee also mentioned the two private members' bills. Its conclusion was that since it supports the government's proposal the private members' bills are to be rejected. There was one dissenting opinion, signed by five of the committee's members. The committee also made a visit to a

[1] Memorandum by the Ministry of Labour 28.5.1996.

work place in a Finnish forest. The reason for this was that forest workers sought to be left outside the new working hours act. Their visit did not lead to any revisions when forest workers were included in the act. The situation for priests was the opposite. They wanted to be included into the new act but were nonetheless left outside.[1]

The committee made some minor changes (of formal character) to the bill and the first reading was based on its report. There were in all 33 speeches by 15 different MPs in the first reading. The dominating issue in the first reading was overtime. The issues of firm level agreements and the influence of interest organisations were also mentioned. The content and wording of the bill were decided in the second reading, according to the report by the committee. No changes were made. In the third reading, there were 20 speeches in all by 15 different MPs. The main issue was naturally whether the bill was to be approved, or rejected by the parliament. Eight of the speakers proposed a rejection of the bill, while seven proposed the bill be approved. The procedure of the voting was to choose between the initiatives by the MPs, or the government bill. There were 113 votes in favour of the bill and 32 in favour of the initiatives. Four voted empty and 50 were absent.[2] It is of great interest to note that in all 48 different MPs supported the initiative but it got only 32 votes at the end. This underlines the superfluous character of plenary sessions and formal voting when matters are decided elsewhere.

A Democratic Deficit?

Formally, it was the parliament that made the final decision on the new law and approved its enactment. Informally, it was the main economic interest groups that together with the government, decided on the content of the law. The minister of labour had even expressed an opinion in the press, where she asked the MPs not to make any changes to the government's bill since the main economic interest groups already had approved the content of the bill. Despite a fairly intense debate in parliament, it made only two minor technical changes to the government's bill. The private members bills were also rejected in the plenary voting.

The question of whether the electoral channel is as subservient to the corporate channel on labour market issues, can only be answered in one

---

[1] Interview with MP 20.5.1998.

[2] Parliamentary protocol 18.6.1996, 2755.

way in this case: yes. When some revisions of labour market issues have become necessary, it is in negotiations between the main economic interest groups, together with the government, where decisions are made. One reservation is needed, however. The electorate channel is not as (totally) subservient as it was in 1968-75, when the so-called Acts of Authority gave the main economic interest groups almost legislative power. One must also bear in mind that it is the parliament that is subservient. Strictly speaking the electorate channel is represented by the government in these issues and the government has enjoyed the confidence of the parliament. The parliamentary principle is thus not totally neglected in decisions on labour market issues in Finland.

An important issue that needs to be addressed is whether the procedures where organised interests have a decisive influence over labour market policy making, automatically lead to a democratic deficit? The deficit-thesis has often been discussed in an EU-context, where its decision making procedures have been seen as lacking in both transparency and accountability. The lack of transparency has mainly been implied in connection to the secrecy of all meetings of the European Commission. The lack of accountability has referred to the limited input by any directly elected representatives of European citizens into law making. As shown in this, and the previous chapters, it is not only in a European Union context where there might be a democratic deficit, but also when it comes to the national parliaments. Before a discussion of a possible democratic deficit of the Finnish parliament on labour market issues, what is needed is an establishment of a set of criteria against which it is possible to assess the deficit-thesis. It is not necessary to discuss the democracy-theme as a whole here, but only to focus on corporate pluralist arrangements as a process. The reason for this is obvious: the corporate pluralist arrangements have not in any way altered the basic democratic rights in terms of free electoral processes, independent public officials, or civil and equal political rights. It is therefore merely a discussion of whether the process of developing working hours regulations would have been 'more' democratic by some other arrangements, than the corporate pluralist ones.

The ideal criteria for a democratic process can be expressed in the following terms. The process must entail effective participation, where all members must have equal opportunities for making their views known. It must involve a voting equality, where every member must have equal opportunities to vote. It must involve an enlightened understanding, where each member must have equal opportunities for learning about relevant alternative opportunities. Finally, it must involve opportunities for the members of a group to exclusively decide what matters are to be put on the agenda.[1] The Committee for Labour Affairs had the formal opportunities to meet all these criteria. In practice, however, these criteria meant nothing, since the issue was decided elsewhere. The same can also be said about the previous chapter. In the committee that prepared the working hours law, the members had formally equal opportunities for meeting these criteria. In practice, however, the central confederations of trade unions together with the government decided the course of events in the end. In this sense the processes were undemocratic. Before jumping to conclusions, one must bear in mind that these ideal criteria remain ideal, and are seldom (never) met in practical decision making.[2] What is needed is therefore more realistic principles.

The first principle should be that the involvement of labour market parties has usually been based on a principle that parties with the most relevant knowledge of the field, should also have access to the decision making arena. As already noted in chapter one, the emergence of the welfare state meant that the tasks and duties the state had to deal with greatly increased. The main economic interest groups were therefore included into the preparatory work of labour market policy making, since they were supposed to possess a good knowledge of the labour market.[3] This pragmatic perspective does only partly fit into more theoretical arguments about democracy and knowledge. According to Dahl, all genuine anti-democratic arguments are based on a superior knowledge.[4] There is no such thing as one or a superior knowledge. There are, however, different kinds of knowledge. Some people may, for example, have superior knowledge about appropriate ends, while others may have superior knowledge of technical means to a given end. For example, the nuclear engineer knows better how to build a nuclear plant than others, because he has the appropriate knowledge about the means of how to do it. This does not mean, however, that he has any better knowledge about the ends, i.e. whether nuclear power is desirable or not. The same can be said about the corporate pluralist arrangements. The organised interests are supposed to have a better knowledge about the means to achieve a desired end. The non-democratic aspect of knowledge is where the ends, or the common

[1] Dahl 1998, 37-38.

[2] Flyvbjerg 1998.

[3] Olsen 1990, 80-82.

[4] Dahl 1989, 63-64.

interest, are defined by someone who possesses knowledge about the means only. [1] Returning to the example with nuclear power, it would be highly undesirable if the nuclear engineer was not only regarded as having the best knowledge about how to build the plant, but was also regarded as having the best knowledge about the necessity of nuclear power.

Comparing this principle to the results of the working hours case study, the overall picture is that the principles of knowledge about means and ends were not met. As shown in the previous chapter the action by the parties taking part in the preparatory work was not primarily based on their knowledge but on a maintenance of interests. They did not, in other words, use their knowledge of the issue as a means only to achieve desired ends, but defined the appropriate ends according to their respective preferences. This also affected the Committee for Labour Affairs since it has had limited possibilities for having any impact on labour market policy making. This case does not therefore comply with the principle of a superior knowledge about the means only.

A second principle that has often been used in justifying the involvement of organised interests, has been that so-called intense minorities, i.e. minorities who feel strongly about their case, should have the opportunity to take part in decision making. The inclusion of these interests would consequently lead to a development of a more stable and consensual democracy. This was also a leading thought in Lijphart's argument on the consociational democracies. These principles boil down to another common assumption, which has been that the state *needs* the participation of organised interests.

Ever since the first incomes policy settlement was concluded in 1968, Finland has been characterised by consensus rather than conflict. Even the abolition of the antiquated rules of qualified majority for parliamentary voting in 1992 did not mean a shift to so-called minimum-winning coalitions. The governments formed after both the 1995, and 1999, parliamentary elections have been extremely broad based, with support from over 70% of the parliamentary seats. In addition, two weeks after the last government was formed in 1999, all the main economic interest groups gave their support for the government. The government's programme for its term in office also included a statement that it seeks close co-operation with the parties on the labour market. In order to run the country without conflicts on the labour market, the government therefore needs the consent of the main economic interest groups. The memory of events from 1993 are

[1] Saward 1998, 25-27.

still fresh, when the government led by the Centre Party had to go back on its intended employer-friendly labour market policy in order to avoid a general strike. This would have greatly damaged Finland's way back from the economic depression in the early 1990s. This does not necessarily mean that consensus is always desirable, a theme which will be discussed in chapter seven. The corporate pluralist arrangements nonetheless largely comply with this second principle, since the parties that are most affected by the policy have been represented by the main economic interest groups.

A third principle that should be met in corporate pluralist arrangements are those that have caused much discussion in the EU-context - the importance of accountability and transparency. Decision making should be non-secret, and the final decisions should correlate with the preferences of the public.

This final principle is less straightforward. The meetings of the committee that prepared the issue were secret and closed to public scrutinisation. It thefore lacked transparency. The accountability of the final decision is more difficult to determine. On the one hand, the organised interests represent a great majority of the labour market - a greater part than voted in parliamentary elections. On the other hand, one may ask whether the central confederations of trade unions represent their members or themselves? Once a member has joined a trade union, he or she seldom leaves. Although the central confederations represent a large number of members, it is most probable that the members stay loyal to the same organisation. Parliamentary elections are held every fourth year and the electorate may therefore voice their opinion by voting differently, or not voting at all. The accountability of the parliament should therefore be higher than the accountability of the central confederations of trade unions, since opportunities and probabilities for abstaining from voting are greater than probabilities for leaving a trade union once becoming a member.

Before drawing too far-reaching conclusions about concepts like accountability and transparency, what is needed is an evaluation of how democratic processes function in modern democracies. It is therefore not so much a question about the level of transparency and accountability, as a question of the rationale of the parties taking part. The most important criteria consequently becomes whether decisions are made as a result of open minded discussions, or as a result of a struggle for a maintenance of interests. This is where the greatest democratic deficit occurs in this case.

If a narrow definition of democracy has been applied when referring to the parliamentary control and power to make new laws, this has not been the case when talking about the working hours law (and labour laws in general) in Finland during the 1990s. If one wishes to change this form of making decisions, it is not primarily the principle of whether to accept their involvement into decision making that is crucial, but the importance of self interest vs. the collective interest. The question is how to liberate oneself from the superior knowledge of one-and-only appropriate ends for the labour market, and look at the problems not only in terms of, for example profit and productivity vs. security and equality. This may be difficult in relation to the self-interest of the decision makers involved. This may nonetheless be an important aspect, if one wishes to solve the problem of democratic deficit where the role of the parliament has been neglected. The philosophical question is one of evaluating whether the process is more important than the outcomes? Do we need parliamentary decisions if the same regulations can be made differently, but with the same results for the individual workers and employers? The question is which kind of institutional arrangements we regard as the most efficient, appropriate and adaptable in solving problems of our time. The parliament has an advantage because it allows for transparency and debates. Agreements made between governments and interest organisations are made behind closed doors and outside any form of public scrutiny. This is not only a problem for the labour market policy making, but a common problem for contemporary Western democracies.

Conclusions

The aim of this chapter was to evaluate whether the parliament was subservient to the organised interests over labour market issues. The answer was without doubt yes. Despite the fact that the parliamentary Committee for Labour Affairs had weekly contacts and held discussions with the parties on the labour market, it did not mean that they could exert any direct influence. These contacts were only informative. As often has been stressed – participation does not necessary mean influence – has been reiterated in this case. The conclusion from the Swedish case of a strong policy-influencing parliament, participating in all policy making stages, is therefore not applicable to the case of the Finnish parliament and labour market policy making. (The growing interest in parliamentary research does not have to mean, as many researchers seem to conclude, that the parliaments have in themselves become more important.)

The parliamentary deficit thesis from the 1970s was contained in this case of labour market policy making. The MPs were to a greater extent members of their parties than members of parliament. The civil servants, and in the labour market case, organised interests, played a decisive role in preparing legislation. The Committee for Labour Affairs still does not have any influence over labour market policy making. This does not automatically mean a democratic deficit, but as turned out to be the case here, the use of superior knowledge by organised interests to define the ends, led to a democratic deficit. The role of the parliament had become secondary, since the parties in the committee that prepared the legislation had reached consensus on the issue, which according to chapter four was merely a rule by the more powerful.

7 Implementation and Public Perceptions – Do Corporate Pluralist Arrangements Matter on the Shop Floor?

Chapter four in this thesis was concerned with the formulation of the working hours legislation, and chapter five dealt with the parliamentary deliberation and decision making. This chapter is concerned with the implementation stage of the new working hours law, focusing on individual workers and employers. The aim is to evaluate whether the corporate pluralist arrangements have had any effect on the implementation of flexible (non-standard) working hours in the 1990s. In the past it is fairly obvious that the corporate pluralist arrangements mattered for the ordinary workers in Finland. The conclusion of the general agreement between the main economic interest groups in 1966, as well as subsequent legislation with a gradual implementation of a 40-hour working week, was naturally of great importance, since Saturday became the second day off, besides Sunday. Other important outcomes of the broad-based settlements were legislative revisions on pensions and annual holidays in the 1970s.

In order to evaluate whether the arrangements still matter in the 1990s, a comparison will be made with a country that differs significantly from Finland on the corporate pluralist 'scale' – the UK. Policy making in the UK, after 1979, has been based on a deregulation of the labour market in order to create more flexibility. The Finnish (and Nordic) labour relations model has on the other hand been characterised by a high degree of centralisation through broad-based incomes policy settlements, as well as the sectoral collective agreements, implemented for whole branches.[1] Both Finland and the UK have had to adapt to similar problems on the labour

[1] Bruun et al. 1992, 247.

market, that is, how to combine workers' rights in the context of greater demands for flexibility by employers. The main objective of this chapter is, therefore, not to evaluate if the implementation of the working hours legislation has been successful or not, but to evaluate how public perceptions of Finnish working hours arrangements differ from the British ones.[1] Is it possible to detect any difference in practices and attitudes on the shop floor towards the implementation of flexible working hours arrangements between a highly regulated Finnish labour market, and an unregulated British labour market?

As noted in the introductory chapter, attempts to introduce incomes policy settlements were not only made in Finland in the 1960s, but also by the Labour government in the UK. Whilst the first broad-based incomes policy settlement was introduced in Finland in 1968, the first two-year settlement had already been in force in the UK between 1948-50. Further attempts to implement incomes policy settlements were made in the UK during the 1950s, but it was not until 1961, that the next settlement was introduced, implementing a so-called pay pause. This settlement was introduced in order to restrain public sector wages, which it also succeeded in doing.[2] After Labour came to power in 1964, the government furthermore introduced a voluntary incomes policy, backed by the creation of a Prices and Incomes Board. There were, however, splits within the ideological left in the UK, as there were in Finland. The British Labour Party was still affected by an internal debate about socialism, and the members of the Trades Union Congress (TUC) were still highly motivated

---

[1] Implementation research has traditionally been concerned with evaluations of the successfulness of various decisions, leading to a somewhat cynical label of it as the pathology of the social sciences. Pressman and Wildavsky noted in their classical study that people should be 'pleasantly surprised when a few good things really happen', since implementation was seen as exceedingly difficult (Pressman and Wildavsky 1973, xiii). Along the same lines, Bardach also noted that 'even the most robust policy – one that is well designed to survive the implementation process – will tend to go awry' (Bardach 1977, 5). One of the reasons why implementation has been viewed as difficult, and scholars often ending up explaining the results of implementation as failures, has been a tendency for them to select cases characterised by: 1) policy areas which have involved several different political levels, 2) social areas with a high degree of variability, 3) issues that have included a considerable freedom of action of the field personnel, 4) issues that have implied a dramatic change and 5) unclear technology for achieving expected goals. The implementation researchers have, according to Rothstein, investigated such programmes that already from the outset have a good chance of failing (Rothstein 1998, 62-64).

[2] Grant and Nath 1984, 169-170.

by class feelings. The Labour policy, based on a need to control unofficial strikes and personal consumption in order to achieve economic growth, did not harmonise with the trade unions' expectations of wage increases.[1]

The conflictual relationship between the Labour Party and the trade unions was accentuated in 1965, when it appeared that the Labour government had to surrender to trade union wage expectations. The government's policy aspirations failed, which led to deflationary measures in 1966. The measures were accompanied by a statutory incomes policy, but by 1968 it collapsed. (In Finland, the currency was devaluated in 1967, but contrary to the UK, the follow-up of the devaluation was more successful.) In addition, the government's break with a commitment to full employment undermined the employers' confidence in it. Between 1965-68, all national incomes policy plans were consequently laid aside. A growing support for the Conservative Party, largely based on anti-union sentiments, as well as strikes in the engineering sector, led to the publication of the White Paper *In Place of Strife* by the Labour government. The Paper stressed the government's power to intervene in unofficial strikes and inter-union disputes. This inevitably led to a split, not only between the Labour government and the trade union movement, but also within the Labour Party. Unofficial strikes in 1969 led to a mass of inflationary settlements and the Labour government's incomes policy had effectively collapsed.[2] The Conservatives regained power after the parliamentary election in 1970, a victory the TUC did not regard as too harmful.

> The TUC does not sing one song when Conservative governments are in power and another when Labour governments are in power. We deal with governments strictly on the merits of the issues.[3]

The support by the TUC for the Conservative government did not last for long, however. The Conservatives introduced an Industrial Relations Act in 1971, based on a theory that the ultimate power lay in the state, and organised interests have to co-operate in order to achieve the national aims set by governments.[4] Both the trade unions and the Labour Party opposed the Act, which led to a reactivation of the relationship between the leaders

---

[1] Middlemas 1979, 434.

[2] Middlemas 1979, 440; Grant and Nath 1984, 170.

[3] TUC-report 1970. Cited in McIlroy 1995, 187.

[4] Middlemas 1979, 443.

of the Labour Party and trade unions, most notably through the TUC – Labour Party Liaison Committee. This committee came to exert strong influence over policy making, and it was regarded as an important factor in laying the foundations for the coming Social Contract 1974-76. Between 1972 and 1974, it was commonly assumed that the UK was ungovernable without the co-operation and acquiescence of the trade unions.[1]

Britain consequently became regarded as more corporatist in character, since the trade union hegemony had broadened and altered the role of the state.[2] Economic policy making became increasingly characterised by tripartism, with a close co-operation between the government, TUC and the Confederation of British Industry (CBI). As a result, a wide range of new legal rights for workers and trade unions were enacted. The political power of the trade unions also increased, since they gained representation in a large number of governmental bodies, and had access to top politicians of all major political parties.[3] In addition, the period between 1970 and 1974 became characterised by a significant wage-drift, as well as a large number of so-called wildcat strikes. For example, the miners' strike in 1972 ended with a pay increase of 17.5 per cent.[4] The increasing influence of the trade unions did not please the Conservative government, who consequently decided to call an election in 1974 on the issue of 'who runs the country'. Labour regained power at the election, and one of its main objectives became closer co-operation between the government and the trade unions.

The development in Finland and the UK in the early 1970s consequently follows the same pattern. As noted in the introductory chapter, the split within trade union movement in Finland was officially overcome by 1969, and most members of the Social Democratic splinter group had rejoined the SDP by the late 1960s. Economic policy making in Finland and the UK was based on broad-based settlements in order to work for moderate wage increases, and thereby lower inflation. In addition, the introduction of these settlements in Finland and the UK increased the influence of the main economic interest groups over governmental policy making in both countries.

In order to be better able to control the labour market and economy, the Labour government again tried to implement a system of incomes

---

[1] TUC 1974, 335. Cited in McIlroy 1995, 188.

[2] Middlemas 1979, 452.

[3] McIlroy 1995, 188.

[4] Grant and Nath 1984, 170.

policy. This time the TUC entered into the Social Contract between 1974-76 with the labour government, and its position as a powerful political factor was thereby further consolidated. According to Marsh (1992), however, the power of the trade unions in the UK had not been as important as often assumed. After 1975, when the government introduced a voluntary incomes policy, the TUC had to agree on restrictive wage increases. In addition, large cuts in public expenditures were introduced in 1976. In 1977, the TUC formally refused to agree on further wage restraints, but nonetheless had to accept their implementation. Despite the fact that the social contract included a number of legislative gains for the trade union movement, it was mainly an incomes policy based on the active co-operation and acquiescence of the trade unions.[1] The positive relationship between the state and the main economic interest groups came to an end at the end of the 1970s. Official and unofficial strikes during a 'winter of discontent' in 1978-79 had rendered the UK ungovernable. Public confidence in the Labour government declined, and the conflicts on the labour market were perceived as the most urgent problem for the country. At the same time, trade unions became increasingly unpopular.[2]

The situation changed in 1979 when the Conservatives led by Thatcher came to power. Trade unions and collective agreements were regarded by the government as the main reasons behind the distortion of free market relations between employers and workers. The political role of trade unions was diminished with the abolition of any social dialogue between them and the government. The government also introduced five new laws, which restricted trade union activity. They were the 1980 and 1982 Employment Acts, the 1984 Trade Union Act and the 1988 and 1990 Employment Acts. The most important result of the introduction of these acts was that the balance of power shifted from trade unions to employers, since sympathy and solidarity actions between different trade unions became virtually prohibited. In addition, trade unions became financially liable for unlawful or illegal action by any of its members.[3] The common assumption was therefore, that the Conservative government led by Thatcher severely undermined the trade union movement. The legislation became sparsely used in practice, however, and when legal action was taken to resolve industrial relations, it often involved laws that had existed prior to the election of the Thatcher government. Indications from shop

---

[1] Marsh 1992, 49-52.

[2] Marsh 1992, 63.

[3] For a complete list of their content, see Sevaldsen and Vardmand 1993.

floors also showed that the history of industrial relations, as well as economic circumstances for individual firms, were more important factors in explaining changes that had taken place since 1979, than the new legislation. Marsh concluded that the Thatcher government had limited influence in transforming policies on shop floors, because of its top-down approach in trying to impose policies, without consultation, negotiation or co-operation.[1] This finding was also observed by Longstreth (1988), who noted that indications from workplace surveys showed, that the basic institutional structures of industrial relations on shop floors had remained intact.[2]

Whilst the development in Finland and the UK represented similarities up to the late 1970s, they nonetheless represent opposites thereafter. Finland has become increasingly characterised by consultation and co-operation between governments and the main economic interest groups, through the continuous conclusion of broad-based incomes policy settlements. The tendency in the UK, on the other hand, has been a shift towards a more deregulated labour market with, for example, a reduction in the role of collective bargaining in wage determination.[3] This has also been reflected in how regulations on working hours have been made in the two countries.

Working Hours Regulations in Finland and the UK

Finland and the UK represent opposites when it comes to working hours. While there are extensive working hours regulations in Finland, the UK has been a country characterised by unregulated working hours. The first general eight-hour working hours law for adults was enacted in Finland in 1917, whilst in the UK, the traditional model has been that working hour arrangements are to be regulated by collective agreements, based on a policy with no interference from the state for those who can protect themselves with collective action.[4] Working hours has consequently been almost completely unregulated in the UK, until the implementation of the EU working time directive in 1998. As noted in chapter three, the government initially challenged the validity of the EU working hours

[1] Marsh 1992, 108; 239.

[2] Longstreth 1988, 420-421.

[3] Robinson 1996, 62.

[4] Hepple 1998, 238.

directive, arguing that it was related to workers rights, rather than health and safety. It was, according to the government, therefore not to be implemented in the UK, since it had not yet in 1993 signed the European Union's Social Chapter. The European Court of Justice (ECJ) nonetheless ruled against the UK government. The new Labour government in 1997 signed the Social Chapter and a new working time regulation was implemented in the UK in 1998.

The latest regulation on working hours in Finland was passed by parliament on the 18th of June 1996, entering into force on the 23rd of November 1996. The outcome of the revised act was that compared to previous ones, it delegated more freedom to set the framework for firm level agreements to the sectoral collective agreements, which are concluded between the national trade unions and employers' associations.[1] As a result of the new act, the following old working hours acts have expired. The Act on Working Hours in Bakeries from 1961, the Act on Janitors' Working Hours from 1970, the Act on Opening Hours for Shops and Offices from 1978, and the Act on Working Hours for Farmers from 1989. The reason for terminating these acts was that they had in many cases become antiquated, as well as not meeting the current needs on the labour market. On the issue of more flexibility, one significant change has been the possibility for unorganised employers, who are not covered by any collective agreement, to conclude agreements at the firm level with their respective workers. In these agreements, it is possible to extend the daily working hours by one hour, on condition that the weekly average amount of working hours does not exceed 40 hours counted over a four-week period. The weekly working hours cannot exceed 45 hours.[2] Opportunities for making more flexible arrangements have also been extended by giving the national trade unions and employers' associations rights to make their own respective collective agreements on a larger number of issues than was possible according to the act before the revision. This development has been justified as a means of providing more freedom to negotiate *(sopimusvapaus)* to the national trade unions and employers' associations on issues like, for example, the definition of working hours and rest.[3]

---

[1] The act itself has also included some statutory flexible arrangements, but only for the employers and workers who are not covered by any collective agreement, consequently comprising around five per cent of the labour market workforce.

[2] Tiitinen et al. 1996, 142.

[3] Tiitinen et al. 1996, 18.

Besides the abolition of the previous acts and opportunities for more flexibility, the new working hours act also includes changes of more formal linguistic character, as well as changes of substance. Examples of changes of substance from the previous acts are the general definition of working hours and overtime, as well as a new regulation on 24-hour rest. In addition, statements on daily and weekly rests have become more unified, and the maximum amount of overtime has been reduced.[1] Working hours are consequently thoroughly regulated in Finland.

As already noted, the only working hours regulation in force in the UK is the one that implements the EU working time directive. The lack of any national UK working hours law can be related to tradition in the UK, where there are no entrenched or social rights to associate in trade unions. (In Finland, the Constitution Act states that everyone shall have the right to form, join or participate in the activities of trade unions.) Certain minimum civil rights included in, for example, the European Convention on Human Rights and the European Social Charter have therefore not been directly enforceable in the UK.[2] There is, however, other legislation that regulates the relationship between employers and workers. The most important of these are the Contract of Employment Rights Act, dealing with individual rights on the labour market, and the Trade Union and Labour Relations (Consolidation) Act, dealing with collective labour relations. Besides the legislation, there are also codes of practice that provide guidance on the application of various statutory provisions.[3] Most conflicts over the implementation of employment contracts are dealt with by the Employment Appeal Tribunal, which was established in 1965. It consists of a legally qualified chairman and two members who represent trade unions and employers' associations. There is no special court in the UK that deals with disputes over collective agreement. Claims against the conduct of trade unions usually go to the High Court, or Court of Session.[4]

In special cases concerning the EU working time directive, matters can be referred to the ECJ.[5] The Court, which is situated in Luxembourg, consists of one judge from each of the EU member states. In principle, they are to be appointed only on the merits of judicial expertise, but in practice

---

[1] Titinen et al. 1996, 17-18.

[2] This situation is about to change with the enactment of the Human Rights Act in 1998, which came into force in 2000.

[3] Hepple 1998, 240-241.

[4] Hepple 1998, 242.

[5] Tiitinen et al. 1996, 283-293.

the political background of the judges has been equally important. The Court is responsible for interpreting the provisions of EU law. It functions like any other national court in the sense that it cannot itself initiate action, but must wait for cases to be referred to it.[1] The court consequently deals with, among other matters, cases where a member state has implemented working hours acts contradictory to what the European working time directive states.[2]

In conflicts over how to implement a specific matter of substance relating to working hours in Finland, an appeal has to be lodged at the district courts. Appeals over the district courts' decisions are lodged at the civil court of appeal, and further appeals ultimately at the Supreme Court. Matters dealt with by these courts are basic disputes over working hour statutes, as for example the calculation of overtime and rest. In cases where there are more complicated conflicts over the interpretation of the act and its statutes, matters are referred to the Labour Court or the Work Council. An example of matters referred to these institutions may be where new circumstances on the labour market raise legal questions on whether they are covered by the working hours act or not. These institutions both consist of representatives for the main economic interest groups and independent experts. They consequently also represent a form of corporate pluralist arrangements.

The Labour Court was established in 1946, and it consists of fourteen members. Besides the chairperson and vice chairperson, two members have to be experts with academic degrees in labour legislation, without any affiliations to the parties on the labour market. There are four members each from the central confederations of trade unions and employers' associations. Two members are appointed by the Ministry of Labour, and two members are appointed by the central confederations of municipal and state workers. The Labour Court solves all legal issues on disputes over the content and interpretation of the work agreement act and the collective agreement act. It also solves all conflicts on the application of firm level agreements. The court, therefore, does not deal directly with the working hours act, except in cases of conflicts over the interpretation of how to implement agreements at the firm level. In conflicts over firm level agreements, it is representatives of the branch union who appear in court,

---

[1] Nugent 1994, 220-229.

[2] Tiitinen et al. 1996, 292-293.

not representatives from the firm level. The court's decision is final and no appeals can be made.[1]

Another institution dealing with these matters is the Work Council. This is a special institution that does not make any formal decisions, but rather gives recommendations on how to solve conflicts. The council, also established in 1946, is a special authority working within the Ministry of labour. It consists of a minimum of nine members. Two of its members (of which one is the chairperson) are experts on labour legislation without any affiliation to the parties on the labour market. A third independent member is a specialist in occupational safety and health and appointed by the Board for Occupational Safety and Health *(Työsuojeluhallinto)*. The rest of the members are representatives of the main economic interest groups. The reason behind the tripartite basis is that the council has to enjoy confidence from all parties on the labour market as a non-partial body. Whilst the reports made by the council are not legally binding but seen as recommendations, in practice, the courts that make the final decision on the legal conflicts have in the main followed its recommendations.[2]

Finland and the UK therefore differ significantly when it comes to working hours regulations, since the UK has un-regulated working hours, except for the implementation of the EU working time directive. The tendency in the UK has also been an individualisation of labour relations. This has meant that, for example, restrictions on women's working hours; men's working hours in bakeries; as well as licensing requirements on employment agencies, have all been removed. In addition, restrictions on

---

[1] Tiitinen et al. 1996, 287-290. Sweden has a similar system to that of Finland. The Swedish Labour Court was founded in 1928. It has basically the same function as the Finnish counterpart, i.e. solves conflicts regarding the interpretation and applications of collective agreements. It consists of seven members: two representing employers, two representing workers and three independent experts.

[2] Tiitinen et al. 1996, 291-292. In Sweden, an equivalent Work Council *(Arbetsrådet)* was established in 1919 with the task of interpreting legal issues and questions of exceptions from legislative statements. The reason behind establishing the council was to make adaptations of legislative statements in different branches easier. It consisted of three members representing the LO, three representing the SAF and three independent civil servants with legislative education. No appeal could be made against decisions by the council. In connection to a legislative revision of the act of occupational safety and health in 1948, the Council was incorporated with the board for occupational safety and health. The functions and composition of the council remained basically the same, however, and it still exists as a part of the Board. (Rothstein 1992, 179-183.)

working hours and conditions for young people have been repealed.[1] As mentioned in chapter three, there are four different levels of collective agreements in Finland. At the national level broad-based incomes policy settlements are concluded as broadly formulated instruments in guiding the national economic and labour market policies. They set the framework for the sectoral collective agreements. These settlements may include statements on flexibility and firm level agreements. For example, the 1991 settlement stated that

> The parties signing this agreements are united in efforts to develop the contemporary system of negotiations in order to enable individual workers and employers to make arrangements at the firm level.[2]

Such statements are to be regarded as broad policy statements and guidelines for how to develop the labour market. The sectoral collective agreements, which constitute the second level, are more comprehensive and detailed, and are important as means in regulating the labour market. This is the level where practical opportunities for flexible and firm level agreements are included. All the agreements at this level must be within the limits set by legislation. The basic principle is that opportunities for more favourable arrangements than the working hours act states are possible in sectoral collective or firm level agreements. Agreements that take away worker's rights granted by legal statutes are illegal. It is then up to the different organisations to take into account the different needs of the enterprises they represent. Collective agreements in the UK have also traditionally played an important role in labour relations. There is, however, an important difference between the Finnish and British collective agreements. Whilst collective agreements in Finland have a legal status (i.e. the parties are obliged to follow them according to law), the British ones are not legally binding, unless explicitly stated.

As noted in chapter two, the working hours regulations in Finland therefore represent corporate pluralist arrangements. As furthermore noted in chapters 4-5, negotiations around the new working hours act took place between the main economic interest groups, and they more or less controlled the whole formulation process. The process of parliamentary deliberation was secondary, since nothing of importance was altered. In addition, problems with interpretations of the legislation are dealt with by

[1] Hepple 1998, 240-241.

[2] Incomes policy settlement 29.11.1991.

the Labour Court and Work Council, both of which consist of representatives of the main economic interest groups. The whole process of working hours regulations in Finland is therefore handled by the main economic interest groups, while in the UK they are more decided at the workplace level. Despite the fact that the two countries have had separate policies on labour market issues, it does not automatically mean that the circumstances on individual shop floors have to differ. Both countries are at present members of the European Union, both countries have implemented the EU working time directive and both countries face the same demands for flexible working hour arrangements.

Flexible Working Hours in Finland and the UK

This section presents an analysis of how widespread opportunities for flexible agreements on working hours have been. The evaluation of sectorwise opportunities for flexible and firm level arrangements in Finland is based on material produced by the Central Organisation of Finnish Trade Unions (SAK), and the Confederation of Finnish Industry and Employers (TT). The material for the UK is based on research by the TUC, the journal Labour Market Trends and analyses made by the Policy Studies Institute (PSI). When focusing on research conducted by the large organisations on the labour market, some problems need to be addressed. For example, in a survey made by the independent Finnish Gallup, an organisation that conducts surveys to order, 71 per cent of the Finnish people thought, that a system where *all* labour market regulations were to be concluded at the firm level, would be harmful for the worker.[1] This survey was ordered by SAK. TT, on the other hand, usually cites surveys, where a majority of the Finns are positive towards extended possibilities for flexible arrangements on *specific* issues, for example working hours.[2] The Federation of Finnish Enterprises (SY), an organisation representing small and medium-size businesses, ordered its own survey of firm level agreements in 1999. According to this survey, 74 per cent completely or somewhat agreed with a statement that, in companies with less then ten employees, the close relationship between the employer and his workers would make firm level agreements possible, without the worker being in a weaker position.[3] Cases

---

[1] SAK tiedottaa 1999.

[2] TT 1998.

[3] SY statement 18.3.1999.

where these organisations would publish material contradictory to their interest, i.e. SAK favouring firm level agreements, and TT and SY favouring collective agreements, are therefore to be regarded as non-existent. They are, after all, interest organisations that are supposed to work for the self-interest of their members.

According to another example, the statistics used by the confederations on the total amount of working hours in the Finnish industry differ significantly. While SAK often presents a figure of 1,717 annual working hours, TT presents a figure of 1,548 hours.[1] The reason for this difference is that SAK uses a concept of so-called theoretical working hours, which includes the annual holiday, while TT uses a figure based on the actual working hours done, excluding holidays. By presenting these materials, it is possible for SAK to argue that the number of working hours is high in Finland in an international comparison, and can subsequently be reduced, whilst TT can argue that they cannot be reduced, since they are already low in an international comparison. The analysis in this section will therefore be completed with material produced by other Finnish institutions, for example, the semi-independent Finnish Centre for Business and Policy Studies (EVA). EVA is the main institution producing material for the business, originally founded by the large business organisations in 1974.[2]

Agreements at the firm level are no new phenomenon in Finland - the first agreements between employers and workers at the beginning of this century were made at the firm level. After the national employers' association (STK, later TT) accepted SAK as an equal negotiation partner in 1940, collective agreements at a national level became more common. In addition, a rapid growth in trade union membership during the 1960s reinforced the position of broad-based incomes policy settlements and sectoral collective agreements. Although trade union membership has remained at a high level in Finland in the 1990s, a third alternative to the broad-based incomes policy settlements and sectoral collective agreements, has become more common, i.e. firm level agreements. For example, the

---

[1] SAK Työelämätieto 2/98; TT Työaikakatsaus April 1999.

[2] There are also other semi-independent organisations like the Labour Institute for Economic Research, which focuses on economic developments and forecasts from the workers points of view. All the central confederations of trade unions are members of the Institute and they also provide for most of the funding available to the institute. Another organisation is the Research Institute of the Finnish Economy, which is an independent organisation focusing on the Finnish financial market and different forecasts.

sectoral collective agreements concluded in 1994, included extensive opportunities for making flexible and firm level agreements. These opportunities were further extended in connection to the broad-based incomes policy settlements for 1995-97 and 1998-2000. In 1996, approx. 63 per cent of all workplaces in industry, 56 per cent in the public sector, and 35 per cent in the private sector implemented some form of firm level agreements.[1] In the UK, more than 50 per cent of all employees worked variable hours every week in 1997, which was more than double the proportions of the mid-1980s.[2] In another study by PSI, one result was that a majority of the British workforce (56 per cent) worked varying hours from week to week.[3] The development in Finland and the UK therefore follows the same pattern, with an increase in flexible working.

The implementation of flexible agreements is not without problems, however. According to Finnish employers, firm level agreements should contain basic issues, such as salaries and working hours, but they should not be extended to issues such as workers' intervention in the management of companies. According to SAK, firm level agreements can be discussed on various issues, for example content and organisation of work, certain arrangements on working hours, as well as equality and training. The only condition for SAK is that the workers' position, as an equal negotiation partner must be safeguarded. SAK therefore regards the shop stewards in companies as playing a pivotal role in developing firm level agreements.[4] This is also why SAK conducted an extensive survey of the shop stewards' position in various branches of the Finnish labour market.

SAK's study from 1996 focused on shop stewards and firm level agreements in seven of its trade union members: the Chemical Workers' Union, Trade Union for the Municipal Sector, the Union of Commercial Employees, the Metalworkers' Union, the Construction Trade Union, the Finnish Media Union and the Finnish Electrical Workers' Union. The study was based on a total of 44 interviews with both shop stewards and employer's representatives in the seven sectors.[5] SAK also made earlier studies of opportunities for firm level agreements in 1994 and 1996.[6] The main conclusion of the studies was that the shop stewards were more equal

---

[1] SAK-reports 1/99, 8.

[2] Labour Market Trends July 1997, 247.

[3] Casey et al. 1997, 16.

[4] SAK-reports 1/99, 4-5.

[5] SAK-reports 1/99, 23.

[6] SAK tutkimustieto 5/96.

to their respective employers in cases where there was greater protection for them included in the collective agreements. There was, however, still a long way to go before complete equality could be reached between shop stewards and employers.[1]

In addition to the survey, SAK conducted further evaluations of how firm level agreements had been implemented in Finland after 1997. When it came to the different sectors of the labour market, all the major ones, i.e. the municipal, state, commercial (trade), graphical (printing), chemical, metal, electrical, and construction sectors, had implemented some kind of firm level agreements. [2] For example, one export-oriented company with 130 employees, producing high-quality cogwheels, had implemented their own working hour arrangements.

> The working hours models outlined in the collective agreement for the metal sector initiated an internal discussion on working hours within the company. When the collective agreement provided opportunities for flexible arrangements, we started negotiations on our own working hour arrangements.[3]

In the commercial sector in Finland, it was also possible to agree on deviating working hours from the national collective agreements at the firm level. According to agreement between employers and workers, represented by their shop stewards, working hours could be a maximum of ten hours daily and 48 hours weekly.[4] Working hours in this sector varied greatly, depending on the company in question.[5] The graphical, chemical, metal, electrical and construction sectors also implemented deviating arrangements from the national collective agreements.[6] In all Finnish workplaces where interviews were conducted, some kind of firm level agreements had been implemented through delegatory statements in the national collective agreements. Opportunities for the most wide-ranging diverging arrangements were implemented at the large, or fairly large, companies. The national employers' association (TT) furthermore presented an evaluation of 14 different industrial companies where new

---

[1] SAK-reports 1/99, 14.

[2] SAK-reports 1/99, 23-24; TT report 1998, 4-9.

[3] TT 1998, 10-11.

[4] SAK-reports 1/99, 25-26.

[5] TT report 1998, 18-19; 26-29.

[6] SAK-reports 1/99.

working hour arrangements had been implemented. The experiences from these companies were without exception positive.[1]

Another indication that opportunities for firm level and flexible arrangements have been widely implemented in Finland appears when viewing what can be called lost opportunities. They are opportunities for firm level agreements included in the sectoral collective agreements, but not implemented by the different branches. In the municipal, commercial and graphical sectors, the different branches had taken all the opportunities presented to them for making firm level agreements. In the chemical sector, there had been more opportunities for flexible arrangements than had been actually implemented. The same could be said about the metal, electrical and the construction sectors.[2] This therefore points to the fact, that the opportunities for flexible working hour arrangements have been widely included in the national sectoral collective agreements. Depending on special circumstances in each branch, flexible working hour arrangements have been implemented when necessary. For example, in certain small workplaces with old-fashioned management cultures in the metal branch, the implementation of firm level agreements had been problematic. The same could also be said about certain branches in the construction sector.[3]

In the UK, flexible working hours had also been implemented in various kinds of companies. Factors that were regarded as important in influencing working hour arrangements, besides the historical development of working hour organisation, were also patterns of demand. This was especially true in the case of the oil industry and hotel branch.[4] The TUC furthermore provided examples from the public sector where flexible working hours had been implemented.[5] In another study by PSI of five different trusts in the health sector, four had introduced flexible working hour practices. The practices included family-friendly working hours, fluctuations in demand covered by overtime, rotational shifts, job-sharing, annualised hours and part-time.[6]

The initial objective behind the revision of the working hours act in Finland, i.e. an introduction of more individual and flexible arrangements on working hours, has therefore to a great extent been implemented on the

---

[1] TT 1998.

[2] SAK reports 1/99, 24-24.

[3] SAK reports 1/99, 31; 34.

[4] Casey et al. 1997.

[5] TUC-report 1998a, 4-6.

[6] Casey et al. 1997, 173-174.

Finnish labour market. This has taken place in a way that has preserved the current hierarchy of making agreements on the labour market, i.e. according to the established way of making agreements at the national level between the central confederations of trade unions and employers' associations. The practices have thereby not demanded any changes in who has the authority to make the decisions. It is furthermore most probable, that opportunities for more flexibility would also have been implemented without any revision of the working hours act. The national trade unions and employers' associations also had great possibilities to implement flexible working hour arrangements under the previous act. The overall picture is therefore that Finland does not differ from the UK when it comes to the implementation of flexibility. It has also been fairly evident in the UK, that legislation, including the EU working time directive, has not constrained the development of flexible working hours.[1] The wishes of employers have therefore been taken into account – what about the workers' perceptions of working hours?

Workers' Perceptions of Working Hours

At an organisational level, the two largest central confederations of trade unions in Finland (SAK, STTK) have worked for a policy of shortened working hours. While shortened working hours in the beginning of the century were justified by health reasons, shortened working hours in the 1990s have been justified as a means in creating employment. The third largest central confederation, representing workers with higher academic degrees (AKAVA) has not demanded any reduction of the statutory length of working hours, but instead a reduction of actual working hours completed. While the statutory length of weekly working hours is a maximum of 40, members of AKAVA in practice usually have around 50 weekly working hours.[2] According to STTK, the normal length of weekly working hours should be reduced from 40 to 35, implemented by a revision of the working hours act. This has been supported by SAK, who also has regarded the length of working hours as being too long. Both central confederations have justified their preferences of shortened working hours as a means in increasing employment, despite the fact that research on working hours has been unable to confirm any positive long-term effects on

---

[1] Casey et al. 1997, 140.

[2] SAK työelämätieto 2/98, 15.

employment by reducing the number of working hours (see chapter three). It is also interesting to note, that it is not only research on working hours that has questioned the impact of shortened working hours on employment, but also ordinary workers. In a survey by SAK from 1997, it asked its members about their opinions on whether a shortening of working hours by two hours daily would have any effect on employment in their respective workplaces. The majority of those who answered the survey were of the opinion that in that case they would have to do the same amount of work, but in a shorter period of time. Only 8 per cent thought that this scenario would create new jobs.[1] According to another survey by EVA, two thirds of the workers thought that unemployment could be reduced only by structural changes on the labour market, for example a creation of new jobs, rather than a sharing of the already existing ones. These opinions also correlated with another survey made by EVA, where the opinions of executive officers were asked. They also regarded a restructuring of the labour market as the most important instrument in creating employment.[2]

There are at least two reasons why the central confederations of trade unions have argued for shortened working hours. One reason is that the contemporary discussion on working hours in Europe has been focusing on a reduction of working hours as a mean in creating employment. The European Trade Union Association (EAY) outlined its policy for the coming years at its congress in 1995. Its goal was a working week of 35 hours. On a longer term, its policy was 32 weekly working hours, divided over four days. These reductions have also been justified by EAY as a means in creating employment.[3] Another reason behind this policy is historical. SAK's standpoint is a logical continuation of its earlier policies. Ever since 1917, when the first legislation on an eight-hour working day was enacted, SAK's policy has been to work for shortened working hours. In the 1960s, a gradual transformation to a 40-hour working week was implemented by general agreement between the main economic interest groups, as well as by a new working hours act. In the 1980s, a further reduction was implemented through the so-called Pekkas-days, when workers doing 40 weekly hours received extra days off. SAK's main argument at their latest congress in 1996 was that employment could only be increased by a division of work, meaning shorter working hours.[4] It is

[1] SAK työelämätieto 2/98, 14.

[2] EVA report 1997.

[3] SAK työelämätieto 2/98, 6.

[4] SAK työelämätieto 2/98, 11.

always easier to hold on to old policies than to create new ones. As shown in the next survey by SAK, these old policies may not necessarily comply with the current attitudes on the labour market.

In 1998, SAK made a survey of 2,000 of its members of which 1,021 replied. The survey was a part of a Gender and Flexibility-project that had been initiated by the British TUC and the Netherlands Trade Union Confederation (FNV). Although the survey was made by reference to its British and Dutch counterparts, any direct comparisons are difficult to make, since the countries differ significantly when it comes to working hours. Statistically, males in Great Britain have among the highest number of regular working hours in Europe, and British and Dutch women work part-time more than their Finnish counterparts. The British and Dutch surveys were furthermore conducted by questioning all employees while SAK made the survey of its members only.[1] Taking into account that SAK represents over 1.1 million employees on the Finnish labour market (of a total workforce of around 2.5 million) this should not be of any great significance, however. Of those who answered SAK's survey, 78 per cent had permanent full-time jobs, 10 per cent had temporary full-time jobs, 10 per cent had temporary part-time jobs, and 2 per cent had other forms of arrangements. Table 7.1 shows a comparison between Finland and the UK on worker's perceptions of their working hours.

Table 7.1 'Do you work more hours than you would like, fewer than you would like, or about the right amount of hours?' (percentage)

	Finland			Britain		
	Men	Women	All	Men	Women	All
More hours	28	32	30	44	29	37
About the right amount	41	33	37	50	63	56
Fewer hours	29	32	31	6	7	7

Source: SAK tutkimustieto 3/98; TUC-report Flexibility at work 1998

On the length of working hours in Finland, 37 per cent regarded the current length as being satisfactory. These are low figures in comparison to

[1] SAK tutkimustieto 3/98, 1.

Britain, where 56 per cent were satisfied with the length of their working hours. In Finland, 31 per cent thought they had too short working hours, while 30 per cent thought they had too long working hours. The main reasons for favouring longer working hours were that they wanted to earn more, or that they were satisfied with their jobs. In Britain, only 7 per cent thought they had too short working hours, while 29 per cent thought they had too long hours. The main reasons why the Finnish workers favoured shorter working hours were that they wanted to be able to spend more time with family and hobbies, or because they felt that shorter working hours would improve their health.[1]

The survey also asked about flexitime and flexible working hours, which is shown in table 7.2.

Table 7.2 'Which, if any of the following ways of working are currently in practice at your main place of work?' (percentage)

	Men	Women	All	Men	Women	All
Flexitime	28	33	30	19	22	20
Working from home occasionally	2	6	4	11	8	10
Working at weekends occasionally to get days off in week	32	38	35	16	15	16
Working longer hours to get extra days off	43	34	39	15	14	15
Annualised hours	22	28	25	17	12	15
Working during term-time, but not during school holidays	3	6	5	4	14	9
Opportunities for unpaid leave	34	38	36	13	16	15

Sources: SAK tutkimustieto 3/98; TUC-report Flexibility at work 1998

Of the SAK members that were interviewed, 30 per cent had some kind of flexitime, while the figure was 20 per cent for Britain. The survey furthermore indicated that Finnish workers had greater opportunities for making individual and flexible arrangements than their counterparts in Britain. For example, 35 per cent of those surveyed in Finland had opportunities for working at weekends and got the equivalent time off during the following weeks. The arrangement did not seem to be a very

[1] SAK tutkimustieto 3/98, 2-4.

appreciated alternative in Finland, however, since only 13 per cent were in favour of this opportunity. The survey on SAK's members also pointed out, that the main reasons for not working normal working hours (9-5), was that the nature of work demanded work to be done at other times. Other reasons were that the workers wanted extra income, or time off during daytime. Of the surveyed, 77 per cent were furthermore completely, or fairly, satisfied with their flexible arrangements, and 71 per cent regarded the working hours arrangements as being acceptable at their respective workplaces.

SAK's survey also pointed to the fact that it was the employer that dictated the working hours arrangements. According to over 50 per cent of those surveyed, the employers nonetheless listened to the needs of the workers. The comparative figure for the UK was 42 per cent. In Finland, 29 per cent had no possibility to influence their working hours, while the figure was 37 per cent in the UK. The Finnish workers also thought that the trade unions' task was to deal with issues related to their member's working hours, but they did not think that this was their most important task.[1] AKAVA's members were an exception, since they regarded wages and working hours as the most important issues.[2] In another interview survey of 1,021 persons conducted by Finnish Gallup, 94 per cent of the respondents thought that the minimum regulations of working conditions had to be made in collective agreements, since individual workers were not equal to their respective employers in wage negotiations. Few of the respondents thought that a new situation, with more flexibility, would have any positive effect on the worker's position in companies.[3]

The overall attitude of the Finnish labour market is that a majority of workers regard themselves as having too much work. In 1998, 54 per cent completely agreed, or agreed with the statement that 'workers have to do too much work at Finnish workplaces and that there are great risks of burn-out'. Two-thirds furthermore regarded the atmosphere at workplaces as becoming worse during the 1990s.[4] This was a common phenomenon in all sectors of the labour market. Of SAK's members, 91 per cent had problems to keep up with the current pace on the labour market. For STTK the figure was 96 per cent, and for AKAVA it was 84 per cent.[5] In Sweden, the current trend on the labour market had also become more stressful and

---

[1] SAK tutkimustieto 3/98, 4-7, TUC-report 1998b, 10.

[2] SAK työelämätieto 2/98, 15.

[3] SAK tutkimustieto hösten 1998, 5.

[4] EVA report 1999.

[5] SAK Tutkimustieto hösten 1998, 4.

mentally tiring. In 1994, 67 per cent of the Swedish workers thought that their work had become more stressful, compared to 61 per cent in 1986.[1] (No data available for the UK.)

These attitudes were not entirely shared by the managers of companies. In 1997, EVA conducted a survey of the attitudes of the executive officers in Finnish companies. The survey was sent to in all 1,984 executive officers, of which 672 replied. The executive officers agreed that there was room for improvement in the interaction between individual workers and employers at workplaces. Around 50 per cent of the executive officers recognised the fact, that there was a great risk for burnout on Finnish workplaces, while the figure was, as noted above, over 90 per cent among workers. In addition, 70 per cent of the executive officers regarded there to be lots of room for improvement when it came to the work morale of Finnish workers.[2] (No data available for the UK.)

While workers in Finland usually made a distinction between workers and employers, the executive officers did not make the same distinction, but instead regarded the interests of employers and workers as being the same, because companies had to stay competitive in order to provide jobs. The most clear difference in attitudes between the executive officers and workers were related to issues on salaries and other arrangements at workplaces. Most of the executive officers were highly critical of a solidaristic wage policy, including gender equality as a part of this policy, whilst workers regarded this as an important feature on the labour market. Another issue, where the opinions of the executive officers and the public greatly differed, was on a statement that '...the market economy has developed in a positive direction'. This was supported by 82 per cent of the executive officers and 35 per cent of the public. On the issue of what factors would work for a 'successful' future, 83 per cent of the executive officers regarded the globalisation of companies as the best way for success, while 79 per cent of the public regarded collective efforts *(yhteisöllisyys)* as the best way to secure a successful future.[3]

It therefore seems that Finnish workers are fairly satisfied with the current working hour arrangements, the most acute problem seeming to be the risk of burnout. Workers are in some cases willing to make individual arrangements on working hours, but in other cases they want the trade unions to take care of matters. The working hours debate is therefore to a

---

[1] SCB report 1998.

[2] EVA report 1997.

[3] EVA report 1997.

large extent dominated by employer's demands for more flexibility in work regulations. This is also reflected in the survey by the Finnish Gallup, where the workers did not want all matters to be decided at the workplace level, although they wanted to have some opportunities for individual arrangements. On the issue of collective security versus individual arrangements, the neo-liberal critics of the welfare state, who advocate a change to a more individual relationship between labour and capital, have limited support from the Finnish workforce. As an indication of this, the Finnish Progressive Party (the so-called Young Finns), who worked for a de-regulation of the Finnish labour market, gaining two seats in the 1995 parliamentary election, lost both its seats in the 1999 election.[1] The most interesting results of the surveys are nonetheless that opportunities for flexible working hour arrangements are, in fact, overall higher in Finland than in the UK, despite the fact that the policy in UK has been based on deregulation of the labour market, compared to the Finnish policy of collective agreements. This raises an important question of whether politics matter.

Does Politics Matter?

This case correlates to a high extent with the implementation literature, since it has underlined the fact that the implementation of flexible working hours is not simply a question of 'doing it'. Pressman and Wildavsky had already underlined this in 1973 by their influential study of the problems surrounding the implementation of an economic development plan enacted by the Congress in Washington for creating employment in Oakland.[2] The core concept of implementation processes according to Bardach, was the concept of control. This control was exercised through bargaining, persuasion and manoeuvring, which later turned into strategies and tactics. The implementation process could therefore be characterised by a number

---

[1] Another indication is Abramson and Inglehart's study between 1990-91 of the importance of post-materialist values, for example aspects like a less impersonal society, ideas count more than money, more say in government and freedom of speech. According to their survey, Finland scored highest of all 40 countries included in the study, with only one in 70 of the respondents choosing no postmaterialist values. In comparison, in Norway, one out of eight of the respondents chose no postmaterialist values. (Abramson and Inglehart 1995, 124-125.)

[2] Pressman and Wildavsky 1973.

of interrelated games, which usually had an adverse effect on a successful implementation. These adverse effects could be characterised as; diversion of resources; deflection of policy goals; resistance to explicit efforts to control administration, as well as a waste of personal and political energies in so-called game playing.[1] Starting from the concept of control, but in a somewhat contradictory fashion to Bardach, Hogwood and Gunn noted that perfect implementation was impossible because the logical preconditions of perfect implementation, like perfect control, were unattainable in pluralist societies. External circumstances affected the implementation processes in directions that were unexpected.[2] By reference to the evidence presented above, it seems that the implementation of flexibility on the British labour market has been less widespread than in Finland. A system with more pluralist labour market arrangements in Britain has therefore had the opposite effect on the implementation of working hours than the centralised system in Finland, where sectoral collective agreements play a decisive role. This would indicate that the Finnish arrangements have favoured the employers to a higher extent than the British arrangements have.

The question of which system reflects the actual needs of the labour market remains open for speculation. On the one hand, it may be argued that the corporate pluralist arrangements in Finland have created a system, where the secondary role of the state has enabled a labour market policy more closely connected to the shop floors. The extensive use of flexible arrangements would serve as an indication for this. On the other hand, it may also be argued that the Finnish system of labour market regulations has worked in favour of the employer's need for flexibility, but at the cost of the workers. As mentioned earlier, a growing number of workers on the Finnish labour market has had problems in keeping up with the current pace, where flexibility is increasing. Depending on which approach is chosen, it may therefore be argued that the implementation of working hours flexibility has been successful, (if focusing on the employers), as well as unsuccessful, (if focusing on the workers). It is, however, close to impossible to provide any definite answer to the successfulness, since individual workers and employers differ in their conceptions of whether flexible working hours are needed or not.

A question of whether the implementation has been successful or not is therefore difficult to answer. The labour market consists of a vast amount of different companies, branches and sectors with their own respective

---

[1] Bardach 1977, 57; 66.

[2] Hogwood and Gunn 1984, 199-206.

demands. Working hour arrangements that are suitable for the multinational telecommunications company Nokia, may not be suitable for the University of Helsinki, and are most probably not suitable for Kovjoki Element, a small construction company in the region of Ostrobothnia. An answer to whether the act has been completely 'successful' or not is therefore not only difficult to answer from the empirical material that is available, but also irrelevant. Unintended consequences may still occur, and unforeseen external circumstances may create new demands and needs for new working hour arrangements. So far, the implementation may be regarded as successful in the sense that the main objectives of the new working hours act have been met to a high extent, i.e. to create opportunities for more flexibility and reduce the number of old working hour acts.

A list of critical variables, developed within the implementation research, therefore becomes rather superficial. For example, according to Mazmanian and Sabatier, such critical variables have been the availability of technical theory and technology, the extent of behavioural change required, financial resources, decision-rules of implementing agencies, socio-economic conditions, support from sovereigns and compliance with policy outputs by target groups.[1] Critics of these kinds of lists have noted that they say nothing about which variables are more important than others.[2] Many of the variables seem obvious and trivial. For example, as Rothstein noted, it is not surprising that programmes that have lacked political and public support, as well as necessary resources, have led to a tendency to failed implementation of the particular decision.[3]

Leaving the question of successfulness aside, the comparison between Britain and Finland poses a more interesting question – does politics matter? Despite a policy of deregulation in the UK and collective regulations in Finland, the outcomes on the individual shop floors are the opposite of what would be expected. Labour market policy based on an implementation of flexibility through sectoral collective agreements in Finland, has been a more successful policy than the policy based on deregulation in the UK, since opportunities for flexible arrangements are higher in Finland than in the UK. This finding can be compared to the evidence from the UK, presented earlier, where the anti-union policy of the Conservative government did not undermine the activities of the trade unions at the shop floors.

---

[1] Mazmanian and Sabatier 1983, 41ff.

[2] Goggin 1983, 331.

[3] Rothstein 1998, 69.

This scenario would have important implications for a common European labour market, since it points at bleak opportunities for the European Union, as an organisation regarded as too distant from the public, to actively have an impact on the labour market. The immediate question is what possibilities there are for a common European labour market policy to have any greater impact on the shop floors. Based on the comparison between the UK and Finland in this chapter, the decisive aspects in developing the labour market would be the character of the labour market itself, not the decisions made at the elite level. Furthermore, ideological, social, geographical, organisational and economical factors most probably play an important role in the implementation of flexible working hours.[1] In addition, these factors also play an important role in the assumption of whether politics at large matter. It may therefore be argued that the implementation of flexibility in the UK has been less widespread than in Finland because of the same factors. Which one of these is the most important remains an open, but decisive question.

Conclusions

The most interesting finding is the obvious paradox between Finland and the UK. The corporate pluralist arrangements in Finland have not impeded the introduction of flexible arrangements, and the arrangements have mattered in the sense that they have in many cases enabled flexible working hours, despite the collective character of Finnish labour market regulations. Compared to the UK, which has had no corporate pluralist arrangements since the 1970s, and actively worked for a deregulation of the labour market in order to create more flexibility, there are in fact more opportunities for flexibility in Finnish companies. The argument by the employers in Finland that collective agreements are a great obstacle against flexibility on the labour market does not therefore get any support from the material presented here. A great variation between different branches is highly probable. The central confederations of trade unions have often been accused by the employers' associations as only wanting to preserve an old model of labour market policy, based on collective agreements. The results of the implementation of working hours nonetheless point to a fact that the central confederations of trade unions and employers' associations have been able to accommodate demands for flexibility with a traditional form

[1] Rothstein 1998, 70.

of collective agreements. It is therefore obvious that the corporate pluralist arrangements have played an important role when it comes to the introduction of flexible working hours.

Another interesting finding in this chapter is the strong sense of collectivity and a solidaristic wage policy among workers. These tendencies were underlined by both SAK's and EVA's survey, and should therefore be fairly accurate. The contemporary discourse in western democracies, largely focusing on competitiveness and productivity of companies, does therefore not have much support among ordinary Finnish workers. A majority of both SAK's and STTK's members also had problems in keeping up with the current pace on the labour market. In this sense, it is not surprising that the trade unions still have the people's trust. A majority of trade union members are satisfied with the work of the central confederations of trade unions, and regard them as being the institutions that are most able to fight unemployment.[1]

Finally, the process of developing the working hours act has now been dealt with at all decision making stages. The need for a revision of the working hours act in order to create more flexibility was to a large extent formulated by individual employers and employers' associations (chapter three). The task of formulation of the act was dominated by the main economic interest groups (chapters four and five), and the statutes of the act have to a high degree been implemented through the sectoral collective agreements between the national trade unions and employers' associations. Problems over interpretations of how the act is to be implemented are furthermore to be dealt with by the Labour Court and Work Council, which consists mainly of representatives of the main economic interest groups and experts on labour legislation. It is possible to state that it was the trade unions that were most successful in the battle of the new working hours act, since the sectoral collective agreements remain the main arena for arranging working hours. (See chapter four). It has nonetheless been the employers who have been the most successful in the implementation stage when opportunities for flexible working hours have largely been implemented. The effects the introduction of flexibility has had on the Finnish workers are not entirely positive.

Returning to the theoretical argument in chapter two, one of the main problems with the corporatist theory was how to define the role of the state versus the organised interests. The question that requires an answer, by reference to this case, is therefore not so much what role the state plays in

---

[1] SAK tutkimustieto, hösten 1998, 11.

tripartite negotiations, but what its role is in bipartite arrangements between the main economic interest groups. Keeping in mind that the public has more faith in the main economic interest groups than in the democratic institutions, this is a question of great importance when dealing with current Finnish labour market policy. This, among other things, will be further dealt with in the next chapter.

8 Conclusions – Consensus and its Side Effects

As noted in the introduction, a changing labour market meant that several labour market issues had been on the agenda during the 1990s. Some of these issues were resolved, whilst others remained unresolved or were still under deliberation. This thesis has represented an issue that was eventually resolved and consequently represents a form of labour market consensus building. The aim of this concluding chapter is to discuss the possible side effects of such a form of consensus building. Three different levels of consensus have been used. The first level, or basic consensus, was reflected in the large coalition governments, in the absence of ideological polarisation between political parties, in the less intense conflicts between producer and consumer interests and in the broad-based incomes policy settlements. The second level, or procedural consensus, was reflected in the abolition of minority veto in parliament, in the increase in parliamentary power at the cost of the president's power, as well as in the labour market rules agreed in the broad-based settlements. The main focus in this thesis has been the third level, or policy consensus, represented by the working hours case.

Side Effects of Consensus?

As noted in chapter one, consensus should be arrived at through consultation, discussion and rule by the 'better argument'. In a context of pluralist values, where diversity is the leading word, the features of consultation, discussion and rule by better arguments furthermore presuppose, according to Sartori (1987), the presence of dissensus. Dissensus, in the forms of opposition and contestation, consequently provides beneficial value to democratic processes, since the aim of dissensus is to bring about changes in consensus, and possibly create a new form of consensus.[1] A consensus without dissensus is therefore characterised by '...a strong ideological colouring which strengthens the status quo and forestalls questioning'.[2]

What appears to be consensual politics may therefore hide some (undesired) side effects. The first one of such side effects can be regarded as a variant of the Marcusian notion of the one-dimensional society. The original thought behind the one-dimensional society was that economic growth has become the only acceptable value in modern Western capitalist societies. This leads to an eradication of political and moral issues from the agenda, by an obsession with productivity and efficiency. This also means that alternative ends are seldom discussed, but debate takes place merely on the means to achieve the predetermined ends. The actors or groups, who are regarded as having knowledge and competence, consequently decide what is to be regarded as rational and appropriate at a certain period of time. Or as Marcuse put it in 1964

> ...contemporary industrial society tends to be totalitarian. For 'totalitarian' is not only a terroristic political coordination of society, but also a non-terroristic economic-technical coordination which operates through the manipulation of needs by vested interests.[3]

When it comes to the corporate pluralist arrangements overall, the inclusion of the main economic interest groups in policy making becomes, according to Held, the modern cathedral, which is supposed to represent an ostensible harmony of society. The pursuit of economic well being and stability forge unity among societal factions, which in turn disengage from class conflict.[4] The state and the organised interests are therefore supposed to co-operate in the name of consensus. This is not an unproblematic relationship, however. If the arrangements mean that the ostensible harmony of a society is arrived at as a consequence of an intolerance of dissensus, then they are not consensual in any true meaning of the concept.

While the first side effect of consensus may be a one-dimensional society, the second side effect relates to the dilemma that the corporate pluralist arrangements create for the democratic institutions of the state. On the one hand, the state needs the special knowledge that the main economic interest groups possess about the labour market. The state also needs their

---

[1] Sartori 1987, 91-92.

[2] Birnbaum 1978, 173.

[3] Marcuse 1964, 3.

[4] Held 1989, 66.

consent in order to secure peaceful labour market conditions. The situation between 1991-94, when the government was led by the Centre Party, represents a good example of this. That government tried to take a more independent role vs. the main economic interest groups in its attempts to curb a deep economic recession, with unemployment figures around 20 per cent. This led to tense relations between the government and the trade union movement, which came to a head in 1993 when the government proposed cuts in unemployment benefits. It also resulted in the threat of a general strike by the central confederations of trade unions. The government had to go back on its intended policies and the relationship between the Centre Party and the trade union movement has remained frozen since then. This has also been regarded as the most important reason for the party being left in opposition since 1995. In practice therefore, it is impossible to leave the main economic interest groups out of processes where labour market issues are discussed. Their participation has become an institutionalised routine. The same time as the state needs their co-operation; it consequently also undermines its own role. The secondary role of the state has been clearly visible in Finnish labour market policy making, where the formulation, deliberation and implementation have in practice been controlled by the main economic interest groups. According to Held again

> Corporatists seem to explain best the much-discussed weakening of formal representative structures, the undermining of the sovereignty of parliamentary bodies, the 'crisis of democracy' in the face of excessive economic pressures.[1]

The corporate pluralist arrangements start to correspond to a classic notion of non-democratic rule – guardianship as a form of rule by experts.[2] This can be characterised as a system where decisions are formulated and discussed among experts, and it is merely left to the democratic institutions to enact their decisions. It is consequently incorrect to regard such a society

---

[1] Held 1989, 66.

[2] In the guardian state that Plato advocated, the rulers should be those who possessed superior knowledge of the policy in question and the ruled were supposed to be regarded as mere amateurs. The underlying notion was that decision making should be based on assumptions of rational certainty where an 'ultimate', or 'perfect' decision that served the interests of a whole community was possible through rational considerations by experts. (Dahl 1989, 52-79.)

as ruled by the people. The argument in this concluding chapter is, therefore, that consensus may lead to a one-dimensional society with an intolerance of dissenting opinions and a government characterised by a rule by experts. The working hours case represents an example of a decision making process when such arrangements have become institutionalised. This thesis has therefore largely focused on the difference between a seemingly consensual outcome in terms of the final working hours act, and the processes behind building consensus on the issue. It is also in the decision making processes where side effects of consensus become visible.

The One-Dimensional Labour Market Policy

When it comes to the working hours case, proposals by the chairperson were not rejected because of acceptable reasons, but were to a high extent rejected because of the main economic interest groups' self interest. Reasoned arguments by the chairperson had in many cases to be withdrawn, since they clashed with the preferences of the organised interests. The process was not equal, in the sense that the employers' representatives were excluded from the final stage of the decision making process, when the government and trade union representatives decided how the final issues of conflict were to be resolved. And finally, reasons persuasive to all were sought, but not found. It is therefore possible to argue that the formulation process in the working hours case has not been conducted according to the principles of good policy making. The main conclusion from chapter four was that it was in the end self-interest and resources that defined the outcome of the issue. The process did therefore not correlate with the general principles of deliberation, but rather with prior norms and requirements of the parties taking part in the process. As furthermore noted in chapter five, the parliament had no voice in the process.

The cases presented in chapter two also support the argument of one-dimensional solutions. The EMU issue left little room for dissensus and opposition to have any impact and the decision was rapidly pushed through parliament. The work reform presented by the Centre Party questioned the importance of the sectoral collective agreements, and was dismissed as such by the SAK. Bearing in mind the problems in reaching an agreement on the working hours act in the committee and working group that prepared the issue of flexible arrangements, the prospects for the Centre Party to make any deep impact on Finnish labour market policy is at the moment to be regarded as slight. The party does not only have to fight its political opponent, (the trade union movement), but also the institutionalised features of corporate pluralist arrangements, where sectoral collective agreements play an important role.

It may therefore be argued, as in the working hours case, that many parts of the work reform became overshadowed by the predetermined end of sectoral collective agreements, which are controlled by the main economic interest groups. Finnish labour market politics has therefore become one-dimensional in character, where such agreements are regarded by the central confederations of trade unions as the one and only possible feature. In presenting alternatives to these, the opposition is accused of trying to return the conditions on the labour market to what they were at the beginning of the century, with no protection for workers. Although the decisions have been made in the name of consensus, it is merely a façade since consensus has been reached by an intolerance of dissensus and alternatives. It is therefore a rule by the more powerful. The real power of the main economic interest groups, in this case the central confederations of trade unions, is their ability to neglect and dismiss dissensus.

The same time as the political development in the 1990s represents both an intolerance of dissensus as well as a one-dimensionality; it nonetheless also represents a stable democracy. The governments have been able to serve their whole terms in office, and strikes have been avoided as a result of the broad-based incomes policy settlements. A survey done by the research institute EVA also pointed to indications that a majority of the public thought that it did not matter which parties were in power – politics would still be the same.[1] Such a development inherits a risk that politics becomes characterised by apathy, where the absence of any clear-cut controversies strengthens the existing power structure. The public becomes detached from the governing of their society, which instead becomes characterised by an increasing role for bureaucrats and other experts.[2] This can in turn lead to a state characterised by guardianship, creating a dilemma for its democratically elected institutions. It is no longer a rule by the people. The working hours case is a prime example of the side effects of such a model of government.

---

[1] EVA 1999.

[2] Birnbaum 1978, 178.

Rule by the Better Argument?

As a principle of government, rule by experts with the best knowledge may sound reasonable. It can be argued that decisions, which concern all, should be made by individuals who know how to best achieve what is good for a society.[1] As has been shown in practice for almost 2,500 years since Plato advocated guardianship, however, the abuse of the concepts of knowledge and common good by minorities and despots has rendered guardianship as a practical form of government highly undesirable. The former communist and fascist regimes in the twentieth century serve as good examples. This does not necessarily mean that the inclusion of experts must automatically be rejected. In modern democracies, where decision making has become highly complex and the tasks for the state have expanded, an inclusion of experts with the best knowledge has become necessary, because the democratically elected representatives of the people cannot possess all necessary knowledge that is required in order to make the best decisions.

Corporate pluralist arrangements, adhering to the principle of experts on labour market issues taking part, are not to be confused with the original principles of guardianship since the arrangements take place in a democratic context. Decisions are made in the context of a democratic rule, but the democratically elected representatives have no real power to make any impact. This was clearly obvious in chapters four and five earlier. It could be argued that the government made the decision regardless of the public on some issues, like for example the EMU. The opinions of the minorities, i.e. those questioning membership were non-accommodated. It was not the public that demanded membership, but more of a policy created by economists within the European Union. (Although a small majority of

---

[1] The underlying assumption of rule by experts as a form of guardianship was that ordinary people were unable to understand and defend their own interests, as well as the interests of societies at large. Government of common affairs should therefore be entrusted to a minority of persons, who had the superior qualifications of knowledge and virtue - characteristics that the majority of ordinary people were seen as lacking. Advocates of guardianship rejected the democratic ideas that ordinary people were qualified to govern themselves. In more abstract terms, the essence of politics was regarded as knowledge about the common good. The search for the common good, and the ultimate truth, was to be delegated to a selected few. These individuals were not only to be completely devoted to the search for truth and what was best for the community, but also do their utmost to achieve that end. The guardians were not allowed to possess any interests or opinions of their own that may have interfered with the common good. In the guardian state complete control over government was therefore delegated to a minority with the superior knowledge. (Dahl 1989, 52-53.)

the Finnish people may support membership, it does not necessarily mean that they demand it.) As noted earlier, the public's preferences shifted considerably in favour of membership of the EMU between autumn 1997 and spring 1998. It could therefore be argued that the public information campaign brought the societal preferences in line with the government's preferences on the issue. If the preferences of the government were clearly sustained on the EMU issue, the outcome of labour market issues is more difficult to determine. On the one hand, the government has needed the assistance of the main economic interest groups in concluding broad-based incomes policy settlements, which were regarded as an important step in creating economic stability on the road to EMU. The government has also needed their assistance as experts on labour market legislation. On the other hand, the government played an important role at the end of the formulation of the new working hour bill, when it decided some issues in favour of the workers' representatives.

It was not only the government that was involved in the process, but also the Ministry of Labour and the parliament. The indications from this case should fairly accurately represent labour market policy making overall, since the actors are the same. It is only the policy issue under discussion that differs. The role of the Ministry of Labour was one of mediation. After the working hours committee finished its work in 1993, the issue was continued in the working group, set up by the government in 1995. The chairperson in the working group, who was a civil servant from the ministry, played the same role as the chairperson in the previous committee. This role was to try and find solutions to the issues where the workers' and employer's representatives did not agree. The chairpersons in both the committee and working group that prepared the issue were powerless, since their proposals were not accepted as such, and they had to present new proposals. The workers' representatives held on to their basic preference with a preservation of the traditional procedure of making arrangements in the form of sectoral collective agreements. The employers' representatives at the same time held on to their basic demand for flexibility. This conflict between the views of workers' and employers' representatives one week before the deadline of the working group led to that the government had to step in and resolve the conflict, largely in favour of the workers' preferences. It is fairly obvious that the decision was in line with the workers' representatives, since the government was led by the Social Democrats. The main economic interest groups therefore negotiated among themselves in the committee and working group on how to decide the working hours issue. They failed to reach an agreement, and it was up to the government to resolve the problem.

The role of the parliament was secondary in relation to the government. The parliamentary Committee for Labour Affairs heard experts on the subject, but did not make any alterations to the proposal for the new working hours act. Despite the fact that the committee had weekly contacts and held discussions with the parties on the labour market, it did not mean that they could exert any direct influence. These contacts were only of an informative kind. As has often been stressed – participation does not necessary mean influence. The parliament enacted the law without changes (except some formal ones). The state therefore became a mediator in the struggle between labour and capital. This does not mean that the state was neutral, since the government took the side of the workers' preferences in the end.

There is, however, more to it than merely a question of who decided the content of the decision and who enacted it. The more important aspect relates to the concept of knowledge itself, and how the actors decided *how* the content of the decision was to be formulated. In order for the process to constitute a reasonable form of government by discussion among experts, the decisions should be made by an assessment of the better or more reasonable argument. As shown in chapter four, it was not primarily the better or more reasonable argument that was decisive, but resources that at the end defined the outcome. The normative foundation of corporate pluralist arrangements as a rule by those with the best knowledge therefore becomes questionable, because it is based on an assumption that knowledge and power are separated. Although the main economic interest groups participate according to their knowledge of labour market issues, it does not necessarily exclude the use of their bargaining strength as large and powerful organisations. One of the most prominent recent authors on democracy has also proposed that

> ...the long-run prospects for democracy are more seriously endangered by inequalities in resources, strategic positions and bargaining strength that are derived not from wealth or economic position but from special knowledge.[1]

By reference to chapter four, it may be argued that the main economic interest groups used their instrumental knowledge merely in order to work for their own respective interests. This comes, after all, not as any big

[1] Dahl 1989, 333.

surprise, since interest groups are supposed to work for the self-interest of their members. Arguments and comments that did not fit into their preferences were rejected. Different alternative proposals made by the chairpersons, who were legal experts on the subject, were not approved as such. The most important issue, i.e. the development of opportunities for making agreements at the firm level, became characterised by incompatible opinions between the workers' and employers' representatives. The participants demanded that certain statements were to be rewritten according to their own respective preferences. The reasonable arguments expressed by the chairpersons therefore had to yield to the power of the workers' and employers' representatives. It was not until the government led by the Social Democrats stepped in and resolved the issues of conflict in favour of the workers that a final solution could be reached. It is therefore possible to say that the main economic interest groups 'misused' their instrumental knowledge of how to develop working hours in the formulation process. At the end it was their self-interest that defined the outcome of the issue. In doing this, they themselves defined what was to be regarded as good for the society.

Reasons that would have been persuasive to all were therefore sought by the chairpersons, but never found. It was a one-dimensional solution where the concepts of flexibility and collectivity became the only accepted ends and could therefore not be questioned or discussed. In Rawls' terms, the representatives of the main economic interest groups were rational agents.

> What rational agents lack is the particular form of moral sensibility that underlines the desire to engage in fair co-operation as such, and to do so on terms that others as equals might reasonably be expected to endorse.[1]

The difference between rational and reasonable agents is that while rational agents lack a desire to co-operate, reasonable agents are able to co-operate with others on terms all can accept. Reasonable agents consequently work for reciprocity where each benefits along with others.[2] This is the reason why it was possible to reach agreements on flexibility in the different sectors on the labour market. The actors who negotiated the sectoral collective agreements were able to function as reasonable agents. As a result, the employers' needs for flexibility as well as the workers'

---

[1] Rawls 1993, 51.

[2] Rawls 1993, 50.

needs for collective security was implemented on the shop floors. As noted in chapter six, the initial objectives behind developing working hours have therefore largely been met after the new working hours law has been implemented. Flexible working hours have been implemented as the employers required, but there is still a strong collective security for the workers, in line with their preferences. The conclusion of sectoral collective agreements took place in different environments and therefore also produced different results. For example, in the metal sector the negotiators normally know what the different companies need, and they most often reach sectoral collective agreements according to these specific needs.[1]

This development starts to correlate with the neo-institutional theory, where the institutional forms of decision making are in themselves to be regarded as important for the outcome. According to the neo-institutional theory, the design of the decision making situation itself plays an important role in altering the self-interests of and action by individuals. This, in turn, means that the institutional setting makes the actors re-define their preferences in order to bring them in line with the collective interest. In the working hours case, this would have meant that the institutionalised way of making labour legislation in committees, where lawyers from the main economic interest groups take part, was to blame for the problems in reaching a solution. The committees did not require any moral logic, since the processes were excluded from the public. Consequently, the parties did not have to argue according to reason, but could keep to their predetermined preferences, without any need for re-defining them. The reason why the committee and working group in the working hours case became characterised by conflict was because of the lack of any so-called rules of reason.[2]

---

[1] Interviews with representatives for employers' associations November 1995.

[2] The so-called rules of reason have been connected to the National Coal Policy Project in the United States between 1977-78. The project was aimed at mediating conflicts between the coal industry and environmental lobbyists. Initially the project was successful when the business people and environmentalists reached agreements on many issues. The government nonetheless ignored most of the agreements the project presented, and it was at the end regarded a failure. The reason why this project is of interest from the working hours case, is that the process of accommodating conflicting views was successful because of the introduction of some negotiating principles that determined the norms of interaction among the participants. These principles, called rules of reason, included among others the following features. Data should not be withheld because it was negative or unhelpful; concealment should not be practised for concealment's sake; dogmatism should be avoided;

Although it complies with the theory of neo-institutionalism, the important issue is whether the institution of regularised relationship between governments and the main economic interest groups matter? They matter in the sense that the regularised Finnish labour market put certain constraints upon actors and define the behaviour by representatives of the main economic interest groups. This behaviour is first and foremost based on self-interest, which is only indirectly defined by the institutional structure. For example, the dilemma for the representatives of trade unions was that the current labour market developments are based on individual arrangements, as opposed to their collective identity. Regardless of which institutional structure is in force, they would still have the same collective identity. The institutionalisation of regularised and close relationships with the employers and governments have enabled them to pursue this identity stronger, than would have been the case in purely pluralistic systems. This does not mean, however, that the identity is necessarily formed or altered by the institutional structure. The same also goes for the employers. Their basic preferences have been individual arrangements, which have complied to the current trends on the labour market, but been constrained by the corporate pluralist arrangements. The concept of normative institutionalism, where institutional norms and requirements determine political behaviour, is therefore not sustained by this case. The antithesis to the normative institutionalism, i.e. rational institutionalism, is more accurate, since mainly the workers' representatives have used the institutional structures in order to work for their self-interest.

The basic problem with corporate pluralist arrangements becomes the exclusionary character of the institutional setting. As long as the development of labour market legislation takes place with only the main economic interest groups involved in the negotiations, the basic underlying conflicts remain unresolved. The problem is, therefore, not the inclusion of these groups into policy making, but the exclusion of other parties, for example politicians, bureaucrats and representatives from individual trade unions and employers' associations. An inclusion of parties other than only the main economic interest groups could consequently work for a more reason-based negotiation culture, where experts from other organisations and institutions would complement the expertise from the main economic interest groups. This would in turn undermine the corporate pluralist modes of interest representation where a few interest groups have access, in favour

relevant data will be disclosed when ready for analysis – even to an extremist opposition; inadequate knowledge will be stated affirmatively, etc. (McFarland 1993, 1-2; 38.)

of a more pluralistic mode with equal rights of representation. As a result, the arrival of consensus as resulting from an intolerance of dissensus could be substituted with real consensus based on, not only rational, but also reasonable argumentation. In a Finnish form of labour market policy making, signified by one-dimensionality and an intolerance of dissensus, this may be difficult to achieve in the near future.

This would also indicate that the current policy style in Finnish labour market policy making radically differs from what has been perceived as a Swedish policy making style. Although it is close to impossible to detect any single policy making style of countries as a whole, there are nonetheless specific certain features that occur more often than others. In Sweden, for example, the policy style has been characterised as deliberative with an extensive use of experts and commissions in dealing with matters. It has also been highly rationalistic and open, with an extensive use of information on the subject and the remiss-system.[1] In Finland, the current policy making style on the labour market can be regarded as more British in character. The dominant British policy making style has been associated with broad consultation, but where specific sets of groups within each policy area have held key positions. Attempts for policy changes within these established policy areas with their distinctive actors have become difficult. This has meant that policy maintenance has been more common than policy change.[2] The problems that the Centre Party has had in having any impact on labour market policy in Finland serve as an example of a similar style in Finland.

Conclusions

The most important conclusion relates to the assumption in the introduction that corporate pluralist arrangements have generated consensus in the working hours case. The conclusion is that it has not been a case of any real consensus, but more a case of an intolerance of dissensus, and thereby a rule by the powerful. The only real consensus has been the conclusion of the sectoral collective agreements where the main economic interest groups were able to take into account both the employers' and workers' preferences. In the working hours committee and working group the actors were more intransigently self-interested than reasonable. The results from

---

[1] Arter 1999, 154; Anton 1969, 98.

[2] Jordan and Richardson 1982, 92.

chapter four showed that corporate pluralist arrangements could not be regarded as ideal forms of deliberation when the preferences of the different parties had not changed as a result of better arguments. The main reason behind the necessity to make this distinction is that power and knowledge cannot be separated.

Secondly, the dilemma for the state rests on the unequal relationship between interest organisational power and governmental reasoning. From this it follows that knowledge or reason is the only source of power the powerless have, and in confrontations between power and reason, power always wins. The main economic interest groups have had more freedom to use and benefit from confrontations, while the experts and parliament have had to base their arguments on formality and legal reasoning. This consequently has led to an unequal relationship between governmental reasoning and interest organisational power. The tripartite relations between the state and main economic interest groups has therefore not been in balance since the corners of labour and capital have decided the content of issues. A justification of corporate pluralist arrangements as a means of including knowledge into the processes therefore becomes questionable. Knowledge is in itself the most important feature of decision making, but when it comes to adversarial relationships between labour and capital, it is soon overshadowed by power. The inclusion of the main economic interest groups cannot therefore be justified by their knowledge of the issue in question, but only by their representative function. The problem with this function is that it is a representational monopoly of certain interests. The same time as it is a representational monopoly, there is a great risk that dissensus becomes suppressed in the name of a consensus, which is defined by the same groups that have the monopoly over interest representation.

The working hours case is therefore an example of decision making proceeding in a context of one-dimensional politics based on predetermined positions. The case should therefore also serve as an example of how decision making in modern capitalist systems functions where predetermined ends cannot be questioned. Knowledge becomes of secondary importance in the struggle for power and dominance. The most important merit of the working hours case becomes its revelation of the practical consequences of consensus. The working hours case has opened up the third dimension of consensus and exposed its underlying side effects for democracy. What has appeared to be consensus between labour and capital, has in many ways been an intolerance of dissensus. From this it also follows, that an institutionalisation of consensus at the first two levels (basic and procedural) does not mean that there is a consensus on the third level (policy).

As noted in the introduction, whilst politics in Finland during the 1950-70s had been largely conflictual in character, indicators from the 1990s point towards a new Finland in a new Europe. Broad-based incomes policy settlements have been implemented during most of the 1990s, and the main economic interest groups have been included into labour market policy making; broad-based governments have been formed since 1995; Communism no longer exist as political force; Finland has become a member in EU and EMU; the parliament and government have gained in power at the expense of the president; and a changing labour market has meant that many labour market issues have been under scrutiny. At a closer inspection, many of these issues reflect current policy making practices in Finland, characterised by one-dimensionality. The work-reform by the Centre Party, the EMU-issue and the question of firm level versus sectoral collective agreements have in Finland to a great extent been predetermined by agreements at the elite-level. This has left the parliament with no voice in labour market policy making. As furthermore noted in chapter six, the current trend on the labour market, including the implementation of more flexibility and competitiveness, has not had entirely positive effects on the workforce. It can therefore be argued that the institutionalisation of the regularised relationship between the government and the main economic interest groups has led to a stress of issues of national interest, at the cost of the interests of ordinary workers and employers. This has been one price to be paid for striving after economic growth and securing a favourable economic development of the country as a whole.

The title of this book was whether the development of labour market legislation in Finland still adhered to corporatist policy making? First of all, although there have been regularised and close contacts between the main economic interest groups and governments, it has not adhered to any distinct forms of corporatism as a concept. The use of the corporatist concept is therefore debatable when it comes to Finnish labour market policy making. In this thesis, corporate pluralism has been used as a 'convenient' term depicting the relationship between governments and the main economic interest groups. Another finding is that there is an important difference between the early broad based incomes policy settlements (1968-early 1970) and the ones concluded in 1990s. Whilst the early broad-based settlements were made in order to improve Finnish welfare system by various social policy legislation, the settlements in the 1990s have been made in order to achieve economic growth, without any extensive social legislative packages. This also confirms the thesis that Finnish labour market policy making has become one-dimensional in character as a means in creating economic growth. Despite the negative features of Finnish labour market policy making, there are also some positive effects like, for example, a labour market with few strikes, governments that have been able to govern, and economic prosperity for a large part of the population.

Appendix

Incomes Policy Settlements in Finland

Settlement	In force	Government (seats in parliament)*
Liinamaa I	1.1.69-31.12.69	SDP,TPSL,Kesk,SKDL,RKP (152)
Liinamaa II	1.1.70-31.12.70	SDP,TPSL,Kesk,SKDL,RKP (152)
UKK	1.1.71-31.3.72	SDP,Kesk,SKDL,RKP,LKP (144)
HL	1.4.72-31.3.73	SDP (55)
Lindblom	1.4.74-31.1.76	SDP,Kesk,RKP,LKP (107)
Miettunen	12.2.76-31.12.76	SDP,Kesk,SKDL,RKP,LKP (152)
Somerto-Oivio	1.2.79-29.2.80	SDP,Kesk,SKDL,LKP (142)
Pekkanen I	1.3.81-28.2.83	SDP,Kesk,SKDL,RKP (133)
Pekkanen II	1.3.84-28.2.86	SDP,Kesk,RKP,SMP (123)
VHS	1.3.86-28.2.88	SDP,Kesk,RKP,SMP (123)
Yhdistelmäratkaisu	1.3.88-28.2.90	KOK,SDP,RKP (122)
Kallio	1.3.90-29.2.92	KOK,SDP,RKP (122)
Tupo	1.3.92-31.10.93	Kesk,KOK,RKP,SKL (115)
Tupo	11.9.95-31.12.97	SDP,KOK,RKP,Vihr,VAS (145)
Tupo	1.1.98-31.12.99	SDP,KOK,RKP,Vihr,VAS (145)

Socialist parties:
SDP=Finnish Social Democratic Party
SKDL=Finnish People's Democratic League
VAS=Left Wing Alliance

Non-socialist parties:
Kesk=Centre Party
KOK=National Coalition
LKP=Liberal People's Party
RKP=Swedish People's Party
SKL=Christian League
SMP=Rural Party
Vihr=Greens

* Government composition at the time of conclusions of the settlements. The parliament has 200 seats in total.

Bibliography

Books and Articles

Abramson, Paul R. and Ronald Inglehart (1995): *Value Change in Global Perspective.* The University of Michigan Press, Ann Arbor.

Aho, Esko (1998): *Pääministeri.* Otavan Kirjapaino, Keuruu.

Allison, Graham T. (1971): *Essence of Decision. Explaining the Cuban Missile Crisis.* Little, Brown and Company, Boston.

Anton, Thomas J. (1969): 'Policy Making and Political Culture in Sweden'. In *Scandinavian Political Studies* 4, 88-102.

Arter, David (1979): 'Social Democracy in a West European Outpost: The Case of the Finnish SDP'. *Polity*, 363-387.

Arter, David (1981): 'Kekkonen's Finland: enlightened despotism or consensual democracy?'. *West European Politics,* 4(3), 219-234.

Arter, David (1984): *The Nordic Parliaments. A Comparative Analysis.* Hurst & Co., London.

Arter, David (1987): *Politics and Policy-Making in Finland.* Wheatsheaf Books, Sussex.

Arter, David (1990): 'The Swedish Riksdag: The Case of a Strong Policy-Influencing Assembly'. In Norton, P. (ed.) *Parliaments in Western Europe.* Frank Cass, London.

Arter, David (1999): *Scandinavian Politics Today.* Manchester University Press, Manchester.

Bardach, Eugene (1977): *The Implemementation Game.* The MIT Press, Cambridge, Massachusetts.

Bercusson, Brian and Linda Dickens (1996): *Equal opportunities and collective bargaining in Europe. Defining the issues.* European Foundation for the Improvement of Living and Working Conditions, Dublin.

Birnbaum, Pierre (1978): 'Consensus and Depoliticisation in Contemporary Political Theory'. In Birnbaum, P. Lively and Parry (eds.) *Democracy, Consensus & Social Contract.* Sage Publications, London.

Blyton, Paul (1985): *Changes in working time. An International Review.* Croom Helm, London, Sydney.

Blyton, P., J. Hassard, S. Hill. and K. Starkey (1989): *Time, work and organization.* Routledge, London.

Bobacka, Roger (1996): *Lagberedning inom arbetsrätten. Avsikter, institutionella arangemang, utfall.* Svenska social- och kommunalhögskolan vid Helsingfors universitet. Universitetstryckeriet, Helsingfors.

Bruun, Niklas (1998): 'Finland'. In *The Regulation of Working Conditions in the Member States of the European Union. Vol.2. National reports*. European Commission, Directorate-General for Employment, Industrial Relations and Social Affairs.

Bruun, Niklas, Boel Flodgren, Marit Halvorsen, Håkan Hydén and Ruth Nielsen (1992): *The Nordic Labour Relations Model.* Dartmouth, Aldershot.

Casey, Bernhard, Hilary Metcalf and Neil Millward (1997): *Employer's use of flexible labour*. Policy Studies Institute, London.

Cawson, Alan (1978): 'Pluralism, Corporatism and the Role of the State'. *Government and Opposition,* 13, 178-198.

Cawson, Alan (1985) (ed.) 'Introduction. Varieties of Corporatism: the importance of the meso-level of interest intermediation'. In *Organized Interests and the State. Studies in Meso-Corporatism.* Sage Publications, London.

Cawson, Alan (1986): *Corporatism and Political Theory.* Basil Blackwell, Oxford.

Christensen, Tom and Morten Egeberg (1979): ' Organized Group - government Relations in Norway: On the Structured Selection of Participants, Problems, Solutions, and Choice Opportunities'. *Scandinavian Political Studies,* 2, 239-259.

Cohen, Joshua (1989): 'Deliberation and Democratic Legitimacy'. In Hamlin and Pettit (eds.) *The Good Polity. Normative analysis of the state.* Basil Blackwell, Oxford.

Copeland, Gary W. and Samuel C. Patterson (1990): *Parliaments in the Modern World: Changing Institutions.* University of Michigan Press, Ann Arbor.

Cox, Andrew (1981): 'Corporatism and Reductionism: the Analytic Limits of the Corporatist Thesis'. *Government and Opposition,* 16, 78-95.

Crepaz, Markus M.L. (1995): 'An Institutional Dinosaur: Austrian Corporatism in the Post-industrial Age'. *West European Politics,* 18, 64-88.

Crouch, Colin and Ronald Dore (1990): 'Whatever happened to corporatism?'. In Crouch and Dore (eds.) *Corporatism and Accountability.* Oxford University Press, Oxford.

Cuvillier, Rolande (1984): *The reduction of working time.* International Labour Organisation, Geneva.

Dahl, Robert A. (1961): *Who Governs? Democracy and Power in an American City.* Yale University Press, New Haven.

Dahl, Robert A. (1989): *Democracy and its Critics.* Yale University Press, New Haven.

Dahl, Robert A. (1998): *On Democracy.* Yale University Press, New Haven and London.

Damgaard, Erik (1992): *Parliamentary Change in the Nordic Countries.* Scandinavian University Press, Oslo.

Damgaard, Erik and Kjell A. Eliassen (1978): 'Corporate Pluralism in Danish Law-Making'. *Scandinavian Political Studies,* 1, 285-313.

Elder, Neil, Alastair Thomas and David Arter (1982): *The consensual democracies? The government and politics of the Scandinavian states.* Martin Robertson, Oxford.

Elvander, Nils (1969): *Intresseorganisationerna i dagens Sverige.* Gleerup, Lund.

Eriksen, Erik (1990): 'Towards the Post-Corporate State?'. *Scandinavian Political Studies,* 13, 345-364.

Esaiasson, Peter and Sören Holmberg (1996): *Representation from above. Members of Parliament and Representative Democracy in Sweden.* Dartmouth, Aldershot.

Flyvbjerg, Bent (1998): *Rationality and Power. Democracy in Practice.* The University of Chicago Press, Chicago.

Furlong, Paul (1990): 'Parliament in Italian Politics'. In Norton (ed.) *Parliaments in Western Europe.* Frank Cass, London.

Garson, G. David (1978): *Group theories of politics.* Sage Publications, Beverly Hills.

Gladdish, Ken (1990): 'Parliamentary Activism and Legitimacy in the Netherlands'. In Norton, P. (ed.) *Parliaments in Western Europe.* Frank Cass, London.

Goggin, Malcolm L. (1983): 'The 'Too Few Cases / Too Many Variables' Problem in Implementation Research'. *Western Political Quarterly,* 39, 328-347.

Grant, Wyn (1985): 'Hints on escaping from the slough of despond: reply to Jordan'. *Scandinavian Political Studies,* 8, 115-117.

Grant, Wyn and Shiv Nath (1984): *The Politics of Economic Policy Making.* Basil Blackwell, Oxford.

Hadenius, Axel (1994): 'The duration of democracy: Institutional vs Socio-economic factors'. In Beetham, D. (ed.) *Defining and Measuring Democracy.* Sage Publications, London.

Hart, R.A. (1987): *Working time and employment.* Allen Unwin, Boston.

Heckscher, Gunnar (1946): *Staten och organisationerna.* KF Förlag, Stockholm.

Heckscher, Gunnar (1958): 'Interest groups in Sweden: Their political role'. In Ehrmann, H. (ed). *Interest Groups on Four Continents.* University of Pittsburgh Press. Pittsburgh.

Heisler, Martin O. (1979): 'Corporate Pluralism Revisited: Where is the Theory?'. *Scandinavian Political Studies* 3, 277-297.

Heisler, Martin O. and Robert Kvavik, (1974): 'Patterns of European Politics: The European Polity Model'. In Heisler, M. and Kvavik, R. (eds.) *Politics in Europe.* David McKay, New York.

Helander, Voitto (1982): 'A Liberal – Corporatist Sub-system in Action: The Incomes Policy System in Finland'. In Lehmbruch, G. and Schmitter, P. (eds.) *Patterns of Corporatist Policy-Making.* Sage Publications, London.

Helander, Voitto (1983): 'Interest Representation in the Finnish Committee System in the Post-War Era'. In Anckar, D. and Helander V. (eds.) *Consultation and Political Culture. Essays on the Case of Finland.* Commentationes Scientarium Fennica, Helsinki.

Held, David (1989): *Political Theory and the Modern State. Essays on State, Power and Democracy.* Polity Press, Cambridge.

Hepple, Bob (1998): 'The United Kingdom'. In *The Regulation of Working Conditions in the Member States of the European Union. Vol.2. National reports.* European Commission' Directorate-General for Employment, Industrial Relations and Social Affairs.

Hernes, Gudmud and Arne Selvik (1979): 'Local Corporatism in Norway'. *Scandinavian Political Studies,* 2, 261-275.

Hewitt, Patricia (1993): *About time. The revolution in work and family life.* IPPR / River Oram Press, London.

Hicks, Alexander (1988): 'National Collective Action and Economic Performance: A Review Article'. *International Studies Quarterly,* 32, 131-153.

Hogwood, Brian W. and Lewis A. Gunn (1984): *Policy Analysis for the Real World.* Oxford University Press, Oxford.

Hörning, Karl H., Anette Gerhard and Matthias Michailow (1995): *The Time Pioneers. Flexible Working Time and New Lifestyles.* Polity Press, Cambridge.

Huuska, Väinö (1968): *Etujärjestöjen painostuspolitiikka Suomessa.* WSOY, Porvoo.

Huuska, Väinö (1970): *Komiteat poliittisessa päätöksenteossa.* Tampereen keskuskirjapaino, Tampere.

Jepperson, Ronald L. (1991): 'Institutions, Institutional Effects, and Institutionalism'. In Powell, W. and Di Maggio, P. (eds.) *The New Institutionalism in Organizational Analysis.* The University of Chicago Press, Chicago and London.

Jessop, Bob (1990): *State Theory: Putting Capitalist States in their Place.* Polity Press, Cambridge.

Jordan, Grant (1981): 'Iron Triangles, Woolly Corporatism and Elastic Nets: Images of the Policy Process'. *Journal of Public Policy,* 1, 95-123.

Jordan, Grant (1984): 'Pluralistic Corporatisms and Corporate Pluralism', *Scandinavian Political Studies,* 7, 137-153.

Jordan, Grant and Jeremy Richardson (1982): 'The British Policy Style or the Logic of Negotiation ?'. In *British Politics and the Policy Process: an Arena Approach.* Allen & Unwin, London.

Jordan, Grant and Jeremy Richardson (1987): *British Politics and the Policy Process.* Allen & Unwin, London.

Jordan, Grant and Klaus Schubert (1992): 'Policy Networks'. *European Journal of Political Research,* 21, 7-28.

Katzenstein, Peter (1985): *Small States in World Markets: Industrial Policy in Europe.* Cornell University Press, Ithaca and New York.

Kavanagh, Dennis (1985): *British Politics. Continuity and Change.* Oxford, Oxford University Press.

Kauppinen, Timo (1994): *The Transformation of Labour Relations in Finland.* Finnish Labour Relations Association Nr 8, Hakapaino, Helsinki.

Knutsen, Oddbjørn (1995): 'Left-Right Materialist Value Orientations'. In van Deth, J.W. and Scarbrough, E. (eds.) *The Impact of Values.* Oxford University Press, Oxford.

Labour Market Trends, July 1997.

Lehmbruch, Gerhard (1979): 'Consociational Democracy, Class Conflict and the New Corporatism'. In Schmitter, P. and Lehmbruch, G. (eds.) *Trends Towards Corporatist Intermediation.* Sage Publications, London.

Lehmbruch, Gerhard (1982): 'Neocorporatism in Comparative Perspective'. In Lehmbruch, G. and Schmitter, P. (eds.) *Patterns of Corporatist Intermediation.* Sage Publications, London.

Lewin, Leif (1994): 'The rise and decline of corporatism: The case of Sweden'. *European Journal of Political Research,* 26, 59-79.

Lijphart, Arend (1968): *The Politics of Accommodation. Pluralism and Democracy in the Netherlands.* University of California Press, Berkeley and Los Angeles.

Lijphart, Arend (1969): 'Consociational Democracy'. *World Politics* Vol. xxi, 207-225.

Lijphart, Arend (1977): *Democracy in Plural Societies.* Yale University Press, New Haven.

Little, C.R. (1985): *The Experience of Work.* Gower, Aldershot.

Longstreth, Frank H. (1988): 'From Corporatism to Dualism?'. *Political Studies XXXVI*, 413-432.

Lowi, Theodore (1964): 'American Business, Public Policy, Case Studies, and Political Theory.' *World Politics vol 16,* 677-715.

Lukes, Stewen (1974): *Power. A Radical View.* The Macmillan Press, London.

March, James and Olsen, Johan (1989): *Rediscovering Institutions: The Organisational Basis of Politics.* Free Press, New York.

Marcuse, Herbert (1964): *One-Dimensional Man.* Beacon Press, Boston.

Marsh, David (1992): *The New Politics of British Trade Unionism. Union Power and the Thatcher Legacy.* Macmillan, London.

Martin, Ross M. (1983): 'Pluralism and the New Corporatism'. *Political Studies, XXXI*, 86-102.

Mazmanian, Daniel A. and Paul A. Sabatier (1983): *Implementation and Public Policy.* Scott Foresman and Company, Glenview, Illinois.

McFarland, Andrew S. (1993): *Cooperative Pluralism. The National Coal Policy Experiment.* University Press of Kansas.

McIlroy, John (1995): *Trade Unions in Britain Today.* Manchester University Press, Manchester.

McRae, Susan (1995): *Part-time work in the European Union: the Gender Dimension*. European Foundation for the Improvement of Living and Working Conditions, Dublin.

Middlemas, Keith (1979): *Politics in Industrial Society: the Experience of the British System since 1911.* Andre Deutsch, London.

Myllymäki, Arvo (1979): *Etujärjestöt, tulopolitiikka ja ylimmät valtioelimet.* Finnpublishers, Tampere.

Nedelman, B and K.G.Meier (1977): 'Theories of contemporary corporatism: static or dynamic?'. *Comparative Political Studies,* 10, 39-60.

Nedelman, B. and K.G. Meier (1979): 'Theories of contemporary corporatism: Static or dynamic?'. In Schmitter, P. and Lehmbruch, G. (eds.) *Trends towards corporatist intermediation.* Sage Publications, London.

Nordlinger, Eric A. (1981): *On the Autonomy of the Democratic State.* Harvard University Press, Cambridge, Massachusetts.

Norton, Philip (1990): *National Parliaments and the European Union.* Frank Cass, London.

Nousiainen, Jaakko (1977): 'Näkökohtia eduskunnan asemasta ja päätöksenteko-järjestelmästä'. *Politiikka,* 2, 113-131.

Nugent, Neill (1994): *The Government and Politics of the European Union.* Macmillan, London.

Offe, Claus (1981): 'The attribution of public status to interest groups: Observations on the West German case'. In Berger, S. (ed.) *Organizing Interests in Western Europe: Pluralism, Corporatism and the Transformation of Politics.* Cambridge University Press, Cambridge.

Offe, Claus (1985): *Disorganized Capitalism. Contemporary transformations of work and politics*. Polity Press, Oxford.

Olsen, Johan P. (1990): *Demokrati på svenska.* Carlssons Bokförlag, Stockholm.

Organisation for Economic Co-operation and Development (1973): *New patterns for working time.* International Seminars 1972-1. OECD, Paris.

Organisation for Economic Co-operation and Development (1986): *Flexibility in the labour market. The current debate.* OECD, Paris.

Organisation for Economic Co-operation and Development (1990): *Labour Market Policies for the 1990s*. OECD, Paris.

Organisation for Economic Co-operation and Development (1992): *New Directions in Work Organisation. The industrial relations response.* OECD, Paris.

Organisation for Economic Co-operation and Development (1995): *Flexible Working Time. Collective bargaining and government intervention.* OECD, Paris.

Pahl, R.E. and J.T.Winkler (1974): 'The economic elite: theory and practice'. in P. Stanworth and A . Giddens (eds.) *Elites and Power in British Society.* Cambridge University Press, Cambridge.

Pekkarinen, Jukka, Matti Pohjola and Bob Rowthorn (1992): *Social Corporatism: A Superior Economic System?.* Clarendon Press, Oxford.

Pekkarinen, Jukka and Juhana Vartiainen (1993): *Suomen talouspolitiikan pitkä linja.* WSOY, Helsinki.

Peters, B. Guy (1999): *Institutional theory in political science. The 'New Institutionalism'.* Pinter, London and New York.

Pierre, Jon and Anders Widfelt (1997): 'Sweden'. In *European Journal of Political Research,* 32, 495-500.

Pressman, Jeffrey L. and Aaron Wildavsky (1973): *Implementation.* University of California Press, Berkeley.

Przeworski, Adam (1998): 'Deliberation and Ideological Domination'. In Elster, J. (ed.) *Deliberative Democracy.* Cambridge University Press, Cambridge.

Rawls, John (1993): *Political Liberalism.* Columbia University Press, New York.

Ricci, David (1984): *The tragedy of political science: politics, scholarship, and democracy.* Yale University Press, New Haven.

Robinson, Peter (1996): *Labour Market Studies. United Kingdom.* European Commission, Luxembourg.

Rokkan, Stein (1966): 'Norway: Numerical Democracy and Corporate Pluralism'. In Dahl, R. (ed.) *Political Oppositions in Western Democracy.* Yale University Press, New Haven and London.

Rothstein, Bo (1988): 'State and capital in Sweden: the importance of corporatist arrangements'. *Scandinavian Political Studies,* 11, 235-260.

Rothstein, Bo (1991): 'State Structure and Variations in Corporatism: the Swedish Case'. *Scandinavian Political Studies,* 14, 149-171.

Rothstein, Bo (1992): *Den Korporativa Staten.* Norstedts, Stockholm.

Rothstein, Bo (1998): *Just Institutions Matter. The moral and political logic of the universal welfare state.* Cambridge University Press, Cambridge.

du Roy, O., J.C. Feys and A.V. Meyer (1989): *Towards a general policy on time.* European Foundation for the Improvement of Living and Working Conditions, Dublin.

Rubin, Marcus and Ray Richardson (1997): *The microeconomics of shorter working week.* Avebury, Aldershot.

Rusanen, Jorma (1994): *Paikallisen sopimisen mahdollisuudet.* Gummerus Kirjapaino, Jyväskylä.

Salminen, Esko (1996): *Vaikeneva valtiomahti? Neuvostoliitto / Venäjä Suomen lehdistössä.* Edita, Helsinki.

Sarfati, Hedva and Catherine Kobrin (1988): *Labour market flexibility. A comparative anthology.* Gower, Aldershot.

Sartori, Giovanni (1987): *The theory of democracy revisited. Part one: the contemporary debate.* Chatham House Publishers, Chatham.

Sartori, Giovanni (1994): *Comparative constitutional engineering*. Second. ed. Macmillan Press, London.

Saward, Michael (1998): *The Terms of Democracy.* Polity Press, Cambridge.

Schmidt, Manfred G. (1982): 'Does Corporatism Matter?'. In Lehmbruch, G. and Schmitter, P. (eds.) *Patterns of Corporatist Policy Making.* Sage, London.

Schmitter, Philippe (1974): 'Still the Century of Corporatism?', *Review of Politics,* 36, 85-131.

Schmitter, Philippe (1979): 'Modes of Interest Intermediation and Models of Societal Change in Western Europe'. In Schmitter, P. and Lehmbruch, G. (eds.) *Trends Towards Corporatist Intermediation.* Sage Publications, London.

Schmitter, Philippe and Jürgen R. Grote (1997): 'The Corporatist Sisyphus: Past, Present and Future'. *EUI Working Paper SPS,* 97/4.

Scholten, Ilja (1987) (ed.): *Political Stability and Neo-corporatism.* Sage Publications, London.

Schumpeter, Joseph A. (1954): *Capitalism, Socialism and Democracy.* 4th ed. Allen & Unwin, London.

Sevaldsen, J. and O. Vardmand (1993): *Contemporary British Society.* Academic Press.

Smith, Martin (1993): *Pressure, Power and Policy.* Harvester Wheatsheaf, London.

Statens Offentliga Utredningar (SOU) 1996: 145.

Statistical Yearbook of Finand 1998.

Strøm, Kaare (1997): ' Rules, Reasons and Routines: Legislative Roles in Parliamentary Democracies'. In Müller, W and Saalfeld, T. (eds.) *Members of Parliament in Western Europe.* Frank Cass, London.

Taddei, D. (1998): *Reduction of working time (a literature review).* European Foundation for the Improvement of Living and Working Conditions, Dublin.

Therborn, Göran (1987): 'Does Corporatism Really Matter? The economic crisis and issues of political theory'. *Journal of Public Policy,* 7, 259-284.

Tiihonen, Seppo (1990): *Hallitusvalta.* Hallintohistoriakomitea ja Valtion Painatuskeskus, Helsinki.

Tiitinen, Kari-Pekka, Tarja Kröger, Esa Lonka and Jaana Paanetoja (1996): *Työaikalaki.* Lakimiesliiton Kustannus, Helsinki.

Trades Union Congress (1998a): *Flexible friends? Case studies of positive workplace flexibility.* TUC, London.
Trades Union Congress (1998b): *The Time of our lives. A TUC report on working hours and flexibility.* TUC, London.
Truman, David (1951): *The Governmental Process. Political Interests and Public Opinion.* Alfred A. Knopf, New York.
Uusitalo, Hannu (1983): 'Incomes Policy in Finland: Economic and Social Effects in a Comparative Perspective'. *Scandinavian Political Studies,* 6, 1-25.
Williamson, Peter (1989): *Corporatism in perspective.* Sage, London.
Winkler, H. (1976): 'Corporatism'. In *Archives Europeennes de Sociologie,* 17, 100-136.

Other Published Material

Collective agreement for the metal industry 1994.
Collective agreement for the paper industry 1994.
Committee Proposal 1992, Nr 39.
Committee Proposal 1993, Nr 2.
Committee Proposal 1993, Nr 8.
Committee Proposal 1993, Nr 11.
Committee Report 1957, Nr 50.
EEC Regulation No 1365/75.
EU Council Directive 93/104/EC.
EU Factsheet (1997). *European Social Policy.*
Eurobarometer 48 (autumn 1997).
Eurobarometer 49 (spring 1998).
EVA (1997): *Raportti työelämän murroksesta – Muutosrohkeutta vai Siilipuolustusta?* [EVA-Report 1997: Report from the changing working life – guts to change or barricade building?].
General Agreement between the main economic interest group 1965.
Government Bill 1965, Nr. 151.
Government Bill 1997, Nr. 98.
Government Programme 1995.
Government Report 19.2.1998.
Government Statement Report 20.5.1997.
Incomes Policy Settlement 29.11.1991.
International Labour Review 1957.
Keskustan työreformi [Centre Party work reform] 30.11.1998.
Labour Market Studies: Finland. 1996. Basic info report by Misep Network, Employment Observatory, European Commission.

Leppänen, Seppo (1998): *Economic Council of Finland.*
Official Journal of the European Communities 13.12.1993.
Parliamentary motions 63; 123; 142/1908.
Parliamentary protocols 15.12.1965; 21.12.1965; 28.12.1965; 2.5.1996; 18.6.1996.
Rehn, Olli (1996): *Corporatism and Industrial Competitiveness in Small European States: Austria, Finland and Sweden, 1945-95.* PhD Thesis, University of Oxford, February 1996.
SAK Julkilausuma 21.11.1998 [SAK public statement].
SAK (1991): *Työaikaselonteko.* [SAK working hours report 1991].
SAK Tiedottaa. *Ay - liike torjuu työreformin – ei paikallista sopimista.* 9.1.1999 [SAK public statement. The trade union movement rejects the work reform – not firm level agreements].
SAK (1996): Tutkimustieto. *Lait, sopimukset ja paikallinen sopiminen SAK: n seitsemässä jäsenlitossa.* 5/96 [SAK Research report. Laws, agreements and firm level agreements in seven member trade unions of SAK].
SAK (1998): Tutkimustieto. *SAK:laisten työaikatoiveet* 3/98 [SAK research report. Working hour preferences among SAK members].
SAK (1998): Tutkimustieto. *Undersökning av arbetsmarknadsklimatet hösten 1998.* [SAK research report: An evaluation of the labour market climate, autumn 1998].
SAK (1998): Työelämätieto. *Työaikaratkaisut 2000-luvulla.* 2/98 [SAK labour market report: working hour arrangements in the 21st century].
SAK (1999): Report. *Local Agreements at Finnish Workplaces.* 1/99.
Statistiska Centralbyrån. 1 . 9 . 1998: *Sysselsätning, arbetstider, arbetsmiljö* (Pressmeddelande) [SCB Press report. Employment, working hours, work environment].
SY Statement 18.3.1999.
TT (1998): Käytännön Työaikaratkaisuja – tarpeen mukaan. [Working hours in practice – When necessary].
TT (1999): Työaikakatsaus huhtikuu 1999. [Working hours overview, April 1999].

Newspaper Articles

Helsingin Sanomat 18.11.1997.
Helsingin Sanomat 10.7.1998.
Hufvudstadsbladet 16.12.1997.
Hufvudstadsbladet 22.11.1998.
Hufvudstadsbladet 9.2.2000.

Interviews

Huotari, Anne. Member of Parliament.
Kantalainen, Kari. Member of Parliament.
Komi, Armas. Member of Parliament.
Leppänen, Seppo. General Secretary, Economic Council.
Lindroos, Reijo. Member of Parliament.
Lonka, Esa. Hallitusneuvos, Ministry of Labour Affairs.
Siimes, Outi. Member of Parliament.
Skippari, Jorma. Lawyer, Confederation of Finnish Technical Salaried Employees (STTK).
Tiilikainen, Reijo. Member of Parliament.
Tiitinen, Kari-Pekka. Professor, University of Helsinki.
Vanhanen, Matti. Member of Parliament.
Virtanen, P. Lawyer, Confederation of Service Employers (PT).

Index

For Product Safety Concerns and Information please contact our EU
representative GPSR@taylorandfrancis.com
Taylor & Francis Verlag GmbH, Kaufingerstraße 24, 80331 München, Germany

www.ingramcontent.com/pod-product-compliance
Ingram Content Group UK Ltd.
Pitfield, Milton Keynes, MK11 3LW, UK
UKHW022126190926
475702UK00013B/1675
* 9 7 8 0 3 6 7 2 4 9 2 0 5 *